THEME PARK PROJECT MANAGEMENT

By Val Usle

COVER AND CONCEPT ART

By Sam Usle

Kimble Creek Consulting, LLC

ACKNOWLEDGMENTS

Walt Disney – Thank you for your Sunday night tours of Disneyland and WED, and your vision of EPCOT. It launched a career that spanned over forty years.

Tino (My Father) – Thank you for what you said in 1975 while we were vaccinating calves in a pasture, "If you want to work for Disney, go get a job at Disneyland."

Jim Lowman – Thank you for giving me the chance to work for RETLAW and drive the monorail.

Frank Stanek – Thank you for the entry point to WED and repeatedly throwing me in the deep end of the pool, particularly the 'Big Picture' end of the pool.

Tom Jones, Jim Thomas, Paul Komer, and Craig Russell – Thank you for all the things you did for me that I never saw you do.

Craig Russell, Jim Thomas, and Jess Kuncar – Thank you for the time you took to review and comment on this book.

Karen DiNoto – Thank you for your editing and comments.

DEDICATION

To Maureen – Thank you for all your love and prayers.

"We didn't have too little.
We didn't have too much. Thank God, we had enough."

Henry Forstner

These are the words at the end of my Grandfather's autobiography. While they speak to his life's experiences, which included the Depression, they can also speak to the reflections of a Project Manager at the end of a tough but successful job.

TABLE OF CONTENTS

GENESIS OF THIS BOOK

My alpha point in theme park development started at age ten watching Walt previewing Disneyland attractions on his Sunday night TV show. Out of this emerged a desire to become one of his Imagineers which quickly went viral, as I traced guest paths on a fun map or shaped the Park out of blocks with a HO train around its perimeter. Years later, after seeing the model of EPCOT at the post show of the Carousel of Progress, the virus became incurable and made things crystal clear – my future had a purpose and it was to help Walt's dream of EPCOT become real.

The Author on Main Street 1960

That future purpose led to mechanical drawing classes in summer school and high school, as well as the pursuit of a degree in architecture. After five rejections, my sixth application to California Polytechnic University at Pomona was accepted to its School of Environmental Design. One of my learnings there was that intellectuals believed they knew what was better for the common Joe than the common Joe. Professors would routinely say, "Why do you want to work for Disney? Disney's not real architecture. Disney's fake, fiberglass stuff." My youthful pushback was, "So, is it safe for me to assume that people like your architecture so much, they are willing to pay to go see it?"

Author with Senior Year Final Project – Mixed Use Complex for Wilshire Blvd

The Author, as College Student and Calf Wrangler in the early 70's

While in college, my foot in Disney's door started in a pasture while vaccinating cattle with my dad. He turned to me and said, "If you want to work for Disney, go get a job at Disneyland." Three days later, I was in front of a Jim Lowman, a recruiter at the Park. The interview was very short.

> Jim: Pointing to my head, "You know…"
> Author: "No problem. If I leave here with a job, the mustache and long hair are gone."
> Jim: "You should also know that there are no jobs open in operations."
> Author: "Again, not a problem. I will sweep your streets, cook your burgers, or put your Pooh Bears on the shelves. My goal is to have a solid work record so that I can transition to WED (Walt's initials that were used as the name for Imagineering) when I graduate."
> Jim: "What?"
> Author: "I will sweep your streets, cook your burgers, or put your Pooh Bears on the shelves. My goal is to have a solid work record so that I can transition to WED when I graduate. I want to be an Imagineer."
> Jim: Looked at me and then picked up the phone, called someone, and inquired if the 'job' was still open. After hanging up, he asked, "Would you like to drive the monorail?"
> Author: "That would be fine."

From that moment I was blessed with the best job at the Park – driving the Mark III Monorail for the Disney family (aka: RETLAW – Walter spelt backward). In return for tearing E-tickets and driving the monorail, I received a starting wage of $2.43 an hour, plus a hands-on education in Park operations and guest flow.

The Author, as Monorail Pilot in 1975

After a little over a year with RETLAW, I came across a Company phone book that listed WED's personnel including their Departments. I jotted down those associated with Architecture, and started cold calling to see if I could arrange a courtesy interview. I worked my way down the alphabet and received polite rejections until reaching the 'J's.' It was there that a Job Captain by the name of Dave Jacobs agreed to talk with me. This got me past the lobby and to a conference room where I shared my sophomore school work along with a bunch of calf barns that I had been doing for my dad's customers. At the end of the meeting Dave informed me that WED did not have any openings at the time. My response was, "That's okay. I don't graduate for two more years. I just wanted to let you know I was in the pipeline coming your way." Between calf barn drawings and the 'pipeline' comment, Dave could not hide the confusion on his face, as I thanked him for the interview.

Fast forward four years later, and I was the equivalent of a Design Manager on Tokyo Disneyland with responsibility to move all of WED's facility, show, and ride docs out the door to the Oriental Land Company. Dave and I were meeting practically every day, as I led design reviews and coordinated with him on drawing content and schedule. I never mentioned our first meeting until his retirement party where I asked him if he remembered interviewing a college kid with calf barns in his portfolio. His response was, "Wait. That was you!"

As graduation approached, I spotted an opening for a Research Analyst at WED posted in the cast break area. The job required someone who could gather, organize, and describe scopes of work for the Estimating team, and it seemed reachable. Frank Stanek, who was the Overall Project Manager for both EPCOT and Tokyo Disneyland, came down to the Park to interview me. This interview went longer than my first with the Company, as I had a full portfolio of school work to share, and could afford to leave the calf barns out. Of all the questions he asked, I only remember the last three.

Frank: "What will you do, if you don't get this job?"
Author: I had given that some thought, "There is an architecture firm called Gibbs and Gibbs in Long Beach. I like their work, and can see myself there."
Frank: "You do understand that this job does not require you to prepare architectural drawings?"
Author: "Yes. My goal is a career at WED, and the Research Analyst position sounds like a great place to start."
Frank: "Okay. Let's talk money. How much are you looking for?"
Author: I knew all my friends were asking for $4 an hour, but I bit my tongue and said, "$5.50 an hour."

Frank: "Well the job pays more than that."
Author: "That would be fine."

Within a week the Studio HR Department called with an offer. I accepted, and soon thereafter, I picked up my diploma from Cal Poly Pomona on Saturday, drove the Monorail for the last time on Sunday, and started work at WED on Monday. I found myself living the dream as an Imagineer.

After writing scopes for EPCOT, Frank assigned me to Tokyo Disneyland where I was among the first wave of talent, and it was there that the seeds of this book really grew. Despite never having built a bird bath or dog house for the Company, Frank took me and so many others* on as apprentices. His approach to making us effective was to surround us with a small team of experienced deputies and his own consistent demonstration of integrity, salted with telling us 'how to act,' and not what to do. Frank's own words best describe his approach.

"I knew that everyone working under my direction was intelligent. They also had a 'grounding' and capability in some skill that had resulted from education and/or experience. What I wanted to give each and every one was the opportunity to expand capabilities, experience, and grow up fast, as both time and capable staff were in short supply. I knew from the opportunities that I was given to be challenged, opportunities to learn something new, roles that went beyond my abilities required me to basically sink or swim. These experiences and opportunities I felt needed to be returned to others, thus when given the chance, I passed them on. It was a 'test' of sorts as well, and not all passed everything that was thrown at them."

"So, 'how to act' was my way of giving everyone a chance and to put the burden on each to learn how best to handle the situation, as opposed to having Frank tell you what to do in each step. Frankly, there was not enough time to babysit everyone. I also knew that not everyone would get it right the first or even the second time; but at least making mistakes meant you were trying to do something."

The Author (center) at the outset of Tokyo Disneyland's construction.

The 'how to act,' was also captured in something we eventually came to call "Frank's Ten Commandments." Ten was more of a title than actual number, as each of us who remember these times carry a slightly different quantity and mix of Commandments. Typical of his Commandments was guidance relative to EPCOT which ran parallel to Tokyo Disneyland's development. To the newbies, both projects were seemingly competing for the same resources. But Frank never gave into, nor let us take hold of that emotion. Instead, the 'how to act,' came in the form of the Commandment, "EPCOT is not a competitor." This was typical of a leadership style that had the goal of creating a cadre of people who could make decisions, and not just parrot a response. He wanted and needed leaders at all levels of the Project who could operate independently within his broad themes, and very exceptionally check-in with him. He also demonstrated more than once that he owned the risk and blowback that came with our errors by putting the shields up when we stumbled, and treated these moments as learning opportunities instead of time in the woodshed.

It was as though we had an invisible copper bracelet on our wrists with the letters WWFD: "What Would Frank Do?" It is important to note that this question did not guarantee success in every application. However, more often than not it worked, and at the end of the day, we could all look each other in the eye. The byproduct of his training ended up producing a group of people who would not try to leverage his name or formal position to advance whatever task was at hand. We stayed away from:

"Frank says…"
"Frank thinks…"
"Frank wants…"

Seeing a major endeavor like the original Tokyo Disneyland from womb to tomb imprints a lot on you with experience being the ultimate teacher. Yes, there was a tremendous advancement on process knowledge and craft, and these certainly sustained me in the years that followed Tokyo, when I co-authored Imagineering's first Project Management Guide and its subsequent revision. Additionally, I was the first Project Manager at Imagineering to take and pass the national PROJECT MANAGEMENT PROFESSIONAL (PMP) certification test. However, I soon learned that, as good as process guides are in creating a framework for human transactions, you can't legislate behavior, and good behaviors are not the natural byproduct of good process. Instead, they emerge from watching great leaders at work. Which is why the content presented here is grounded in the, "How to act," instead of, "What to do."

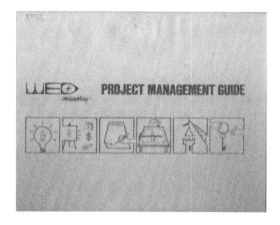

WED's first Project Management Guide, co-authored by the Author.

Thus, the pages that follow are not full of process insight, such as work breakdown structures, matrix management org charts, earned value formulas, pull planning techniques, or building information modeling. If your goal is to be a PM, you should have an understanding of all of these and a command of some. That's because improved behaviors without good process are not enough to deliver a project well, and bad process or a lack of process framework are the equivalent of settling for gas station sushi.

Nor is this book a regurgitation of 'Frank's Ten Commandments' (If you want a copy of those – see Frank). Additionally, like the common sense that got us to the moon with more slide rules than computers, the pages here are not technology dependent. Instead, you will find an expansive look at <u>leadership wisdom</u> that grew from Tokyo and the projects that followed it. This wisdom is offered to help offset drama typically found in the themed entertainment industry.

Every project and team are different, and there are no guaranteed solutions presented, but it is hoped your read will reduce 'coulda, woulda, shoulda' hindsight that would follow your own 'practice' of leadership in developing theme parks, resorts, Expos, World's Fairs, and other thematic designs.

The Author's Forty Year Service Award

*A measure of a leader's success is the success of those they grew, and among Frank's many apprentice hires were Craig Russell and Bob Weis – who respectively have run or are running Walt Disney Imagineering.

INTRODUCTION

This book is the class you never had in college. It focuses on helping you be a Leader who knows that your duty is to serve others at whatever level your role might be.

Project Management is not a person, but the human glue holding the Team together around the Artist and the Big Idea. While the focus of this book is on the Project Manager or PM, the reality is that in a matrix organization, every player at the intersection of a pool of professionals and the Project is in essence a project manager (small p and m). The individual at that node has the responsibility to organize and channel the talents of their home base to serve the needs of the Project in a fixed amount of time and money. Other than scale of responsibility, that charter bears little difference to that of the PM's.

The Project Management concepts presented are rolled-out under the context of a theme park, land, or attraction in its earliest and most fragile part of life – the transition from an artistic dominant endeavor to a Project with multi-disciplined interests. This time is dangerous for the newly minted Project, as the end state is binary. The Artist's vision will either survive, as the product of a multi-disciplined team, or never meet its intended audience and die, as a piece of unbuildable or unaffordable art in a corporate vault. But don't get hung up on the possibility of negative outcomes, as not every project should or can be built.

The design and construction of large, themed environments is a complicated venture dependent upon the successful translation of art into executable design. Given that Project Teams rarely have enough time, money, or resources – the human physics employed by the leadership will make life easier or harder for everyone. Poor behaviors added to this high-pressure environment can twist relationships into a reality show where the only learning gained from self-inflicted drama is, 'what not to do next time.'

On the reciprocal side, simple success means a Project Team has been able to embed technical, code, and functional requirements into the Artist's Big Idea without killing its compelling nature or having to overload the path to success with a punitive number of caveats. In fact, to overcome the issues that will arise against the Project's viability, the Big Idea must get even more compelling. To this end, this book presents people-solutions to people-problems that can help move a project beyond just simple success by making the Big Idea bigger.

It is not predestined that every Project Team will detour into soap opera antics. However, avoidance of that swamp is no accident and typically results from healthy behaviors demonstrated by leadership starting day one and consistently repeated in the open. Just as a team that has soured on itself breeds more of the same, one that has little tolerance for picking at itself can develop that attitude, as an expectation within its ranks. Instead of being the stars of a reality show, these teams would be better cast on a cooking program where recipes for success (and not car wreck relationships) are what hold the audience's attention.

The birth of a Project has been selected, as the timeframe for the concepts presented, because getting things moving is difficult, and this period is also when the biggest decisions are made. Teams succeeding in passing through this gauntlet of viability will naturally carry their behaviors forward. Thus, Best Practices adopted early are easier to flow into the downstream life of the Project. With this in mind, Best Practices are the currency of this book. And like fiction, the book's buffet table of Best Practices is organized into three parts – a beginning, middle, and end.

- Part I or the 'Beginning' is the Project's birthday when **ART BECOMES A PROJECT** and a multi-disciplined Project Team is mobilized to join the Artist in advancing the design and vetting critical issues.
- Part II or the 'Middle' is all about **DISCOVERY** and follows the Team after mobilization and into the main body of their work as they artistically, technically, and commercially vet the BIG Idea.
- Part III or the 'End' is all about, **"ARE WE THERE YET?"** It gathers the Team's conclusions and presents them before the Benefactors. The latter will either move the Project to the next round of work, or shut it down and return everyone to their homeroom.

Each Part is built with chapters that start with context or background, cite related sources of drama that can arise from within or outside the Team, and end with suggested Best Practice wisdom to eliminate or dampen the drama. And as you work through each chapter, don't be surprised if you find it has bearing on other Parts of this book or could be useful in downstream phases.

TERMS AND DEFINITIONS

To organize the key concepts presented, the terms and players described below are used throughout the book.

- **THE BIG IDEA:**
  - This is the vision of a compelling thematic environment that emerges from the Blue Sky Phase and has the potential to exceed its intended audience's expectations.

- **THE ARTIST(S):**
  - This is the creator, author, and birth parent of the Big Idea.

- **BENEFACTOR(S):**
  - These are the executives who initially sponsor the Artist's work, and if they find it compelling, commit the organization to flesh-out the early vision of the Big Idea by mobilizing a Project Team to iterate it through a gauntlet of technical, functional, and commercial hurdles.

- **DESIGNERS:**
  - These individuals blend art and technical problem solving. Designers partner with the Artist to translate the vision into executable solutions. These individuals may be artists, show designers, architects, or engineers. If the lead Artist does not continue to the end of the Project, Designers serve as paladins to bridge the Artists intentions with the realities of construction and manufacturing.

- **LATTE BENEFACTOR:**
  - This is the PM's and Artist's champion from the Benefactor community. 'LATTE' refers to the three of them routinely sitting down to share coffee, status, and issues.

- **OBTW:**
  - Oh, By The Way...

- **OPERATORS:**
  - These are the people who live with the Project <u>forever</u>.

- **PROJECT MANAGER (aka - PM):**
  - This is the leader tasked to facilitate the Team's Project Management Process, which includes defining objectives for the Big Idea and removing barriers to the Team's work. They also keep an eye on, and remind everyone of, time, resources, and capital constraints.
  - PMs provide Benefactors with a single belly button for status of work underway and results.

- **FUNCTIONAL LEADERSHIP (aka – pm):**
  - These leaders are responsible for a specific pool of professionals assigned to the Project (e.g., AE staff or ride engineers or show designers). Their designation as lowercase 'pm' infers their duties and roles are similar to that of the PM.

- **PROJECT MANAGEMENT:**
  - This is the process of planning and executing an idea within specific quality, scope, financial, and schedule goals.

- <u>PROJECT TEAM (aka: the Team):</u>
  - o The Team is a temporary business set up by the Benefactors for the purpose of determining whether the compelling Big Idea can survive technical and financial requirements without becoming a Small Idea.
  - o Everyone charging the Project is a member of the Team, whether internal or external to the company. This includes the Operators, who eventually get the 'keys to the car,' and live with the Project for the remainder of its life.
  - o Unlike most businesses, the Team is a temporary organization that is eventually dissolved with the cancellation or opening of the Project.

Time Travel Attraction Concept

PART 1 - ART BECOMES A PROJECT (AKA: The Project's Birthday)

Blue-Sky Definition:
- As adjective: Not yet practical or profitable
- As used here: The brainstorming process that leads the Big Idea with few constraints placed upon it.

Our story starts with an Artist having convincingly pitched a Big Idea born in Blue Sky to Benefactors, who conclude it is worth a discrete round of funding to reveal its potential and risk. Though sideline advice to the Artist may have been available in Blue Sky, more than likely there has been minimal ownership of technical, code, functional, cost, and schedule issues up to this point. And by default, the Artist may have been the closest thing to a PM during Blue Sky.

To confirm the Big Idea can be delivered with tolerable risks and a profitable outcome, Benefactors charter and set in motion a Team led by a PM. However, there is no guarantee they will achieve the desired outcome, and in fact, more ideas go to their graveyard than get built. As was said in the movie, THE GODFATHER, "It's not personal. It's strictly business."

Advancing the Artist's vision does not stop with a 'Project' being declared, but now the go-forward creative iterations have to be blended with other purposes brought to the table. That process depends on grounding the new arriving talent with the expectations of the Artist and supplementing that viewpoint with the goals of the Benefactors. This can't start without a successful mobilization of the Team which PART 1 addresses.

Projects are temporary businesses. This one is now open for business.

1.1 – TALENT: THE GREATER AMONG EQUALS

Background:

The first person to join the Artist coming out of Blue Sky will most likely be the PM. Both need to form a visibly effective partnership. They cannot afford to just tolerate each other and put up a false veneer of trust and cooperation.

Sources of Drama:

- If the Artist and PM cannot reconcile their respective roles, this gap in understanding their opposite's purpose can unleash an endless stream of visible and behind the curtain conflict.
    - A PM believing, they are in charge can lead to their prescribing scope reductions. Artists are told to cut the dancing bear scene, instead of being asked for candidates for possible cuts.
    - An Artist believing, they are in charge can lead to cost and schedule commitments being treated as a low priority. This cuts the legs out from under the PM, but it won't be long before the Benefactors realize that robust vetting of the commerce and technical sides of the Big Idea is not happening. Welcome or not, that's when they will inject themselves into the Project.

- It is very difficult for the Team not to get caught up in arguments between Mom and Dad (aka: The Artist and PM). And like the classic house divided, opposing tribes will form, as people take sides with the dreaded 'them' assigned to the opposing camp.

Best Practices:

- If the Benefactors have not established, or the company has not institutionalized what the relationship is supposed to be, then the Artist and PM will need to reach an agreement that allows both to be effective in their work.
    - First, such an agreement should be premised on the reality that there is plenty of work for both.
    - Second, both parties need each other if the Big Idea is going to get built.
    - Third, if it were not for the Big Idea, there would be no Project and no PM.
    - Fourth, up to this point, the Artist has more experience and time on the Project than the PM. In fact, during Blue Sky, the Artist <u>was</u> the PM.
    - Fifth, the Artist is the closest thing to a Walt Disney, Steve Jobs, or Elon Musk that the Project has. Yes, these individuals are business people, but at their center of each is a creative engine closer to the Artist's genome than the PM's. Given the PM would have difficulty saying no to these gentlemen, deferring to the Artist should be a natural inclination.

    Bottom line: In the absence of an institutionalized relationship between the Artist and PM, the care and protection of the Big Idea trumps the PM's desire to be the leader of all things. While the Artist and PM may speak in public about their partnership, the greater among equals is most likely the Artist.
    - Caveat here: The Artist is obliged not to hinder the development of reliable cost and schedule forecasting, nor can they hide bad news.

- If the Artist and PM cannot reach agreement on the nature of their partnership, then the Benefactors have to be solicited to quickly settle the matter. The Benefactors will get to be somebody's 'bad guy' on this matter.

OBTW:

If the PM is superior to the Artist, that means they can drive or significantly influence the creative content, which is equivalent to two people trying to hold the pencil.

1.2 – TALENT: HIRING SOMEONE TO MANAGE YOURSELF

Background:

If the Project is a one-off for the organization, or the depth of the company's bench does not include a Project Management function or suitable candidate, you could be looking at a consultant to fill the PM seat.

Sources of Drama:

- There are difficulties in securing talent from the outside:
  - First, it is easy to underestimate the time needed to solicit, interview, extend an offer to, and onboard a candidate.
  - Second, with the Project in its infancy there is no guarantee it will go forward, and hiring a great person for what may be a very temporary assignment is difficult.

- It is hard for any consultant to match the 'sea legs' of those in a well-established organization.
  - The financial system and traditional content of each phase can be very different from the outside PM's experience.
  - The consulting PM may not have the sensitivities to the Artist's vision of the Big Idea, and put more weight on its commercial aspects at the cost of ensuring that its compelling nature is not lost. Or on the flip side, the consulting PM may overly defer to the Artist who ranks high in the Owner's organization.

- If presented with the question, "Who do you work for?" they will most likely respond with the name of the individual who signed their employment contract. The rare consultant PM responds with, "The Audience."

Best Practices:

- Hiring a consultant to manage yourself should be your last choice, not the first. However:
  - If you have exhausted available alternatives, then spend the time needed to pick the consultant well, as it is hard to change horses once the race has started.
  - Most of the time, good people are not waiting on benches. Instead, the talent you want is probably finishing a job. Also, remember that, if the candidate is good, their host organization is probably pitching them to clients beyond your organization.
  - It is not unreasonable to secund the PM from their company for the term of the Project to minimize home office loyalties.
  - Everyone in the Owner's organization is obliged to help the new PM be successful and 'grease their learning' relative to the Big Idea and the organization's institutional approach to work.

- When using a consultant Project Manager, Benefactors cannot afford to limit their oversight to periodic milestone reviews. Someone from the organization needs to mentor the consulting PM, and check-in with a frequency that does not micromanage, but at the same time does not let the job get too far down the road.

OBTW:

FYI. The draft for this chapter drew some of the toughest remarks. Emphasis was on, "Never do this!"

1.3 – TALENT: OF HOGS AND NEWBIES

Background:

"Good judgment comes from experience, and a lot of that comes from bad judgment." Will Rogers

Sources of Drama:

- Staffing with average performers or on a bell curve of past performance (e.g., staff being cast range from mediocre to outstanding) would seemingly give you average results, but multiple critical paths running through the Project at any point in time do not tolerate average very well.

- On the other hand, being a talent hog becomes a bad thing if you wait too long for key staff to become available.

Best Practices:

- Would you want to drive an average car, take an average vacation, or live in an average house? Probably not. So why treat your project to average people? Answer: There is no reason to do so, and it's not a form of greed, if you want to be a talent hog. The greater question is whether you have the time to wait for good talent to come off other projects. Patience here can be rewarded, but establish a realistic limit in terms of the wait time you can absorb.

- Most of us started as entry level talent, and someone saw potential in us which led to a chance to prove that we were equal to their expectations. We may not have been the first choice, but those that brought us into projects did so to fill staff gaps. In doing so, they used a <u>bell curve of experience</u>.
    - Onboarding the inexperienced (again - those who display potential) contributes to healthy design iteration by harnessing idealism, energy, technology (e.g., the latest software tools), and viewpoints not diluted (or jaded) by past experiences. Recognize that great talent can come with little or no experience.
    - Consider including in the mix those with tremendous promise, as opposed to moderate performers with experience. However, the casting of inexperienced talent needs to be deliberately managed by stretching them within the boundaries of their potential. This isn't about micromanagement of the newbie or fitting humans with training wheels. It is about carefully selecting those you intend to figuratively throw in the deep end of the pool with the proviso that someone is standing nearby to make sure they don't drown.
    - And Mentors, don't forget to be the kind of boss you had... one that put up the shields for you, when you inadvertently stepped on the toes of others by actions derived from inexperience. You wouldn't have survived without your boss doing things on your behalf that you never saw, and those you mentor cannot survive without you doing the same.

- Lastly, do not be afraid to hire someone who is smarter than you. There are a lot of those people out there.

OBTW:

Another problem that comes with taking on experienced people who are 'average' is that you can end up doing their work for them, and you do not have time to do their job and yours.

Additionally, if in the end one of your pms (small p, small m) is average in your mind or that of others, you need to set expectations early. This is best started through a frank discussion with their functional manager, who should have a bias to defend their people (e.g., ask for a second chance for the team member). Once you and the functional manager are on the same page, both of you need to sit down with the individual and share your collective expectations. If the Project gets approved for another phase of work, both of you should sit down again at the end of the current phase, and provide a report card. If there is a significant shortfall, it is not unreasonable that the individual be changed-out before the start of the next phase.   A 'third chance' is difficult to entertain at that point.

1.4 – TALENT: PMs WITH ZERO RUN TIME

Background:

It is not unusual for the person with the least amount of experience on the Team to be the PM.

Sources of Drama:

- Team members rolling their eyes behind the back of the PM display a body language of disrespect that will not stay private for long. Once in the open, it can permanently damage relationships.

Best Practices:

- The PM is there to help and serve you. You have no less a duty to them.

- Tolerate their mistakes, just as they should tolerate yours.

- Serve as a counselor and mentor to them on your aspect of the business.

- Compliment them when you catch them doing something well, and let their boss know when it is an item of significance.

- Enjoy the youthful optimism, passion, and energy the newbie PM brings to the job. It probably mirrors your own from earlier days.

- Quash discussions outside of the PM's presence in which people joke about or put them down. Have their back.

- When they pitch a strategy or approach that has not worked previously, don't start a rebuttal citing all the times it failed. Instead, ask pointed questions derived from the learnings of those past experiences. Help them move toward your viewpoint through education.

OBTW:

If the best practices above do not move you, then just remember, your newly minted PM may be running the company someday. Stranger things have happened. So, don't be the one who says to yourself years later, "I should have been nicer to them back then."

1.5 – TALENT: THE ART OF CAT HERDING

Background:

Project Management has been described as an exercise in herding cats. This is a cliché that should die, as cats can't be herded.

Sources of Drama:

- At the start of any job, a PMs suddenly finds they have a barn full of cats – aka: a bunch of scary smart people who have been there/done that combined with a gaggle of new people who say, "Watch this!" Yes, the PM can just surrender and open the barn door to let them roam at will. But it will be hard to get all that wasteful Brownian Motion back in the bottle.

Best Practices:

- Have an informal lunch with each cat and ask them to identify a couple of things they want to do on this project. Find one or two that align with your vision and become a cheerleader relative to those specific endeavors. Then expand the conversation to share your thoughts on a few key things you would like them to do.
  - Cats and people do have something in common, and it is their desire for independence which can go hand in hand with fostering ownership of next steps, outcomes, and issues.
  - Converting independence to ownership can encourage the growth of low maintenance team members who want the independence to solve problems, before the greater Team dives in to 'help them.'
  - Cats love to do something when they think it's their idea. Help your cats to reach that conclusion.
    - Harry Truman said it best, "It is amazing what you can accomplish, if you do not care who gets the credit."

OBTW:

There is a reason you can't walk cats, so don't try to put them on leashes (i.e., micromanage them).

1.6 – BENEFACTORS: TOO MANY CHIEFS

Background:

"No shortage of decision-makers does not mean you get decisions." The Author

Sources of Drama:

- Benefactors are sometimes organized as a committee of executive peers with no discrete leader. This adds one more brick to the PM's shoulders, as it falls on them to serve as a surrogate leader that provides the focus for any engagements between the Benefactors and the Team.

Best Practices:

- Recognize that your Benefactor audience may span the Myers Briggs spectrum. That is, some easily absorb information presented and can quickly provide feedback, while others may want to study it first and present their opinions and questions later. Attempt to provide information before the meeting so the latter personality types have a chance to assimilate it.

- If you look around the room, and cannot figure out who is in charge among the Benefactors, you are. Albeit, you are a facilitator, and not a decision-maker.
  - o As you work the room, avoid telling your bosses how to do their jobs, but help them discover the path you see by sharing its pros and cons compared to alternatives.

- The absence of questions should not lead you to conclude everything is well. Take the time to go around the room and probe for individual's concerns, recommendations, or comments. Take note of those with the best comments or questions.

- Avoiding 'death by committee' requires the Artist and PM to informally press for a Benefactor to step up as their champion. This individual does not need to be the most senior person, but instead, is the one most interested or with the most at stake in the Project. When you find such a person, start building a relationship that extends beyond milestone meetings. The Artist and PM having coffee with their champion every few weeks is the way to jump start the Latte Benefactor relationship.

- The PM has to establish who approves the Team's progress and final work.
  - o Minimize progressive layers of approval (e.g., get approval of this Committee, then that Committee, and then...)
  - o Consolidate formal/final approvals into one, or hopefully no more than two sessions.

OBTW:

A sign of good health is when either the Artist or PM can't make the Latte session, the other is okay with them meeting with the 'Latte Benefactor' alone. If the Artist and/or PM cannot tolerate the other meeting the Latte Benefactor alone, it could be a sign of a shortfall in trust between them.

1.7 – BENEFACTORS: STRETCH GOALS ON STEROIDS

Background:

"A 747 landing on an aircraft carrier is a helluva thing to see, but you would not want to be on either vessel."
The Author

Sources of Drama:

- It is extremely easy for Benefactors to mess up a project by launching it with impossible goals or requirements. These are the stories of the lunch table where colleagues hear the chronic woes of those trapped in a seemingly slow-motion car wreck of a project in which Benefactors:
    - Present goals with scope, schedule, or budget far short of historic norms.
    - Require too many options/variants to be studied in the time available. For example:
        - Let's look at Option A with the base scope minus X
        - Let's look at Option B with the base scope minus X and Y
        - Let's look at Option C with the base scope minus X, Y, and Z
        - Let's look at Option B opening in three phases.
    - Want too many meetings with the Team to review progress without providing enough time between the meetings to progress the work.
    - Launch the Project with a serious overextension of the organization's resources or capabilities.
    - Are never available or chronically change the dates for milestone exchanges.

Best Practices:

- The short honeymoon period at the outset of mobilization gives the Artist and PM a chance to caveat ownership of the Project in whole or part. This leverage isn't about saying 'no' to the Benefactors or outright rejection of the assignment's objectives. Instead, it is a diplomatic pushback that makes the Benefactors part of the solution with conversations that start with the PM saying:
    - "We can do this, if you (the Benefactors) approve sole sourcing the ride system."
    - "We can do this, if you (the Benefactors) can receive deliverables A and B after the milestone review."
    - "We can do this, if you (the Benefactors) grant me the authority to approve overtime."
    - "We can do this, if you (the Benefactors) can make the future expansion decision earlier."
    - "We can do this, but if you (the Benefactors) don't want to spend the money on this critical mockup upfront, then it needs to be recognized that the technical vetting of the Project will be incomplete."
    - "We can do this, if you (the Benefactors) make yourselves available to meet during the yearend holidays."

OBTW:

Do not dismiss the importance and brevity of the honeymoon period.

Additionally, some caution is advised here. Not every stretch goal you are given is 'on steroids' because doing hard and/or complex things is part of the PM's job. Before you jump to the conclusion that the Benefactors' ask is too much, you need to have done your homework on the issues at hand.

1.8 – BENEFACTORS: PROJECT MERCURY

Background:

Before we could land on the moon, we had to figure out a way to get to and from earth orbit.

Sources of Drama:

- It is extremely easy for Benefactors to mess things up by directing the Team to use untested strategies or bleeding edge technology. By not giving them a vote on the matter or time to adequately vet the technology, the Benefactors may:
    - Unintentionally end up owning more of the new approach than the Team.
    - Introduce passive resistance in the ranks of the Team, as individuals feel their doubts or concerns were ignored. This results in their quietly giving less than full support.

Best Practices:

- <u>Don't just salute and blindly accept having to take on what no one has done before</u> – break down the challenges into bite size chunks.
    - When President Kennedy announced we were going to the moon, it was a Big Idea loaded with risk. But that risk was deliberately mitigated by a step by step process that broke the task into three programs: Mercury, Gemini, and Apollo. Each program's flight was progressively harder, and each flight's results adjusted the next one's approach to the problem.

- If the Team has significant doubts on the new approach, it is the PM's responsibility to see if the size or footprint of the new approach can be reduced into a more manageable 'walk before you run' chunk similar to the Space Program. This requires the Team to isolate an early portion of the Project from its main body and run the equivalent of the 'Project Mercury' against it without putting the entire project at risk. The amount to be exposed to the new approach has to be large enough to vet its pros and cons, but small enough that the entire Project is not at risk. Pitch this strategy to the Benefactors with the intent that your 'Project Mercury' will let their next project go to 'Project Gemini' status and stand on your shoulders in a more expansive use of the new approach.

- To fight passive resistance by the Team to the new approach, find someone who is a true believer/subject matter expert. Tag that person, as the 'Coach,' but ensure they are not the presumptive fall guy or gal. This is done by the Artist and PM providing visible support of their effort.

- Leave mental room in your head (and schedule) for lots of 'discovery,' as you move away from the shore of traditional means and methods.

OBTW:

Progress in this industry means technology is being adopted soon after its invention. This introduces significant technical discovery which consumes time and money, as the Project seemingly finds itself taking two steps forward and one back. Additional layers of discovery (and risk) come into play, when the new technology is being applied in ways that were not anticipated by its original creators.

1.9 – BENEFACTORS: "WE'RE FROM THE GOVERNMENT, AND ARE HERE TO HELP"

Background:

Benefactors have deep opinions and want to share them.

Sources of Drama:

- Benefactors advice (aka: pressure) for a newly minted Team can include:
    - "Keep your Team Spartan-like."
    - "We can't afford what's on the drawings. You need to get down to the target."
    - "Don't do what Project X did."
    - "I am worried about this or that, and you should be too."
    - "Your job is to beat the historic numbers."
    - "This is what keeps me up at night."
    - "You've got to be lean, lean, lean in your work."
    - "Don't do things the old way."
    - "There is a hard date that this Project must open by."
    - "I don't want this thing to become a science project."
    - "There is no more money. So, don't come back to the till."

Best Practices:

- Veteran Team members expect to hear these messages delivered with institutionalized repetitiveness. However, to the extent that Benefactors are sources of advice, Teams should not be shy about asking for more specifics or help on things clearly above their pay grade.

- Benefactors have long memories and are more than willing to share them with you. When they do, make sure they move beyond the description of any end state failure they are recalling and into the causation. Have them include, "What would they have done differently?"

- The best advice a Team can get is not advice at all. Instead, it starts with a Benefactor's question, "How can we (or I) help you?" or a Benefactor saying, "Here is my cell phone number. Don't be afraid to use it, if you find yourself in a corner." If this is not offered freely by benefactors, seek it.
    - This is the minimum relationship you should establish with your Latte Benefactor.

OBTW:

If you are able to establish a Latte Benefactor, never BS them. A Benefactor's BS Meter is always on. You should expect them to pitch some hard questions, and then they will listen closely for hemming and hawing on your part or that of the Artist.

1.10 – BENEFACTORS: FALSE STARTS

Background:

New PM, "I wasn't there with the Benefactors, but this is what I heard came out of the meeting."

Sources of Drama:

- If significant items related to mobilization or overall goals are unclear, it blindsides the Team. If the PM is faced with taking guidance from a meeting never attended, the Project will be hamstrung by missing pieces of the puzzle that originate from:
    o   Someone saying something the others did not hear
    o   Someone hearing something that no one said
    o   Someone saying something important that others elected to ignore
    o   Someone saying something important that others elected not challenge
    o   Elephants in the room that no one talked about
    o   Competing Big Ideas for the same site
    o   Questions as to whether the Big Idea is highest and best use of land or capital
    o   Artist obligations to change part of the Big Idea based on Benefactor input
    o   Any inferences that the Big Idea presented is just a holding card for something very different that comes later
    o   Grossly overstating the viability of the underlying technology.

    Any of the above is an inescapable landmine for the Team and derails healthy iteration because no one can solve a problem if they don't know it exists. Ignorance of critical information leads members of the Team to find themselves working a project that differs from their colleagues. It also puts them out of sync or at odds with Benefactor expectations.

Best Practice:

- If not present at the approval meeting, the PM should convene the Benefactors to read back what they believe are the Team's goals and Project sensitivities.

OBTW:

If you are unable to reassemble the Benefactors to clarify issues, leverage the Latte Benefactor for the clarity.

1.11 – BENEFACTORS: DESIGN COMPETITIONS

Background:

Some Benefactors believe playing the organization off against itself or against an outside entity is healthy, as it is a way to ensure the Big Idea does not leave anything on the table. Or, they know that under a different hand, the Artist's vision of the Big Idea would be different and perhaps better.

Sources of Drama:

- In an organization where these dual paths can be afforded and the strategy of induced competition is the norm, it is less awkward. But for organizations where it is exceptionally used, it comes across as Machiavellian at a minimum, as the original birthparent of the Big Idea may perceive the situation to be a cage fight with another team. To them the situation is very Darwinian, as only the strong seemingly win.
    - Under these circumstances, the other team might not believe that all critical information has been or is being shared with them.

- This added stress can create some real 'deposit your 5 cents here for Lucy' moments among the Team, and the Benefactors who launched the competition may find themselves serving as camp counselors.

- If the Artist or PM lets the other team get "into their head," that new resident steals time from their Big Idea. And fear of competition can also slow their own work down by pulling the cone of silence over their own Team's work in order to hide it from their competitor.

Best Practices:

- As in the field of athletic competition, good sportsmanship should be the dominant behavior.

- When your Team is trying to win the 'King's favor,' spend the time making your Big Idea better instead of spending time on the cons of your competitor. That being said, make sure you understand your Big Idea's cons. Address them as part of the design problem you faced, and present your solutions to mitigate them.

- In the end, the raw strength of your Team's Big Idea and the efforts to validate it should drive the Benefactor's judgement, and not which team was the most polished. Don't lose sight of the content objective of your work by dwelling on what the other team is or isn't doing.

- Benefactors who launch such competitions need to be more available to the Teams to serve as referee and advocates of everyone. They should also set ground rules that prohibit the hiding of information.

OBTW:

For efficiency purposes, some of the players on your Team may also serve on the competitor's. Resist the temptation to use them as your spy, and don't treat them as though they the other team's spy.

1.12 – BENEFACTORS: MORE PAPER = LESS RISK

Background:

The subject here is elective paperwork, and not that required by law.

Sources of Drama:

- It is extremely easy for Benefactors to contribute to waste on a project by directing or inferring that the Team produce specific paperwork. In doing this, the Benefactors can create:
    - Pyrrhic paperwork that costs more than the issue being tracked or served by it
    - Dilution of the Team's focus and efforts
    - Work that no one on the Team expects will be read by the Benefactors.
        - This equates to not taking the Benefactors or their requirements seriously.
        - Authors of such paperwork will treat outputs as something to be checked-off and not carefully considered.

Best Practices:

- Do not test the Benefactor's 'BS METER' by skipping paperwork they are expecting.
- Assume the paperwork requirements emerged from a legacy need or rigorous consideration. That being said, if something is not applicable or bears little applicability, pitch the reduction in paperwork well before reaching its due date.
    - It is tempting not to produce the excessive paperwork to see if anyone notices it missing. However, it is better to challenge the Benefactor's expectations on specific paperwork at the outset, rather than testing if they notice it missing in a meeting.
        - Example: "You'll note that we do not plan to do Appendixes K, M, S, and T, as there are no known issues, or there is very little applicability to this Project."
    - Candidates for cuts include 'nice to have' paperwork which will quickly become visible, as it slows down the generation and collection of critical paperwork.
    - Like a law no longer needed, don't be shy about proposing sun-downing paperwork that is no longer useful and/or costs more to produce than the cost of the issue being vetted.

OBTW:

Paperwork you consider superfluous and a candidate to cut is a solid topic for discussion with the Latte Benefactor.

1.13 – BENEFACTORS: LOOKING OVER THE HORIZON

Background:

Benefactor guidance can be weak in identifying the specific work that <u>has</u> to follow the currently funded effort. Government agency interfaces, deep utility planning, site investigation, and mockups are just a few of the areas that may have prerequisites the Team needs to anticipate.

Sources of Drama:

- The Team assumes the Benefactors know more than they do about tasks that would follow the currently funded efforts.

Best Practices:

- During mobilization, it is incumbent that the PM's work plan includes:
    - Identifying critical path activities that follow the end of the currently funded efforts, as well as associated prerequisites that need to be accomplished within current funding.

- The PM should also flush-out the Benefactor's intentions by having a clear understanding of what will happen if the Project is given a GO. Will it:
    - Pause briefly?
    - Go on a long hiatus?
    - Immediately launch into the next round of efforts?
    - Execute major real estate transactions, infrastructure construction, or technology commitments?

OBTW:

By the end of this phase, <u>the PM will know more about the Project than any other person on the planet</u>. The Benefactors expect this, and also expect that they have conducted all the necessary reconnaissance for the Project's go forward path.

1.14 – TEMPERAMENT: THE ART OF THE POSSIBLE

Background:

"Always with the negative ways." Oddball in the movie KELLY'S HEROES.

Sources of Drama:

- The dirty little secret everyone knows is that more Projects are cancelled than built. And most of the Team has been to that rodeo before, where their best efforts were for naught. This can jade some, as it is always easier to be a critic than a doer, and this can tempt people to:
    - Avoid healthy iteration by waiting for 'the real project' to show up so that they don't have to redo their work again and again
    - Spread the seeds of their doubts
    - Not work the problem hard enough to discover solutions that overcome their doubts.

- It is worth mentioning that the flip side of Team members not believing the Project is viable is blind optimism or desperation. This is displayed in pursuing solutions that are doable, but not practical. Blind optimism can also come when Team members' big issues can be kicked to the next phase.

Best Practices:

- Being a Team member means <u>you have an obligation to be an advocate and contribute your best efforts</u> toward establishing the Project's viability. However, if leadership tries to mandate best effort with a, "Thou shalt..." it will only mask the critics' view of reality, and draw a weak 'yes' from them. Given this, soft sell becomes the necessary approach.
    - Everyone has to eat, and breaking bread 'one on one' is an informal and simple way to begin turning those with doubts into advocates. A PM can say, "Grab your lunch, I'll grab mine, and let's meet on the patio. I want to hear about your concerns, and share some of mine."
        - You'll note that the discussion starts with the leader listening.
        - Do this with everyone, and not just the visible doubters.
        - This tool is available five days a week.

- Blind optimism and desperation look the same, and are another source of downsides for the Team. However, before these can be addressed with some of the tools elsewhere in this book, you need to recognize the symptoms. Examples include:
    - "The design works, as long as the building does not literally grow another inch bigger."
        - You should not be fighting for this margin of space, when you just came out of Blue Sky.
    - "We can make the multi-level walk-through work, if we have a dozen escalators each with a dedicated operator at the top and bottom of each floor."

- o "Fire truck lanes are not important at this point."
- o "Guest evacuation from the ride is way too hard to figure out right now."
- o "The Big Idea is so good, that there is no doubt that the Benefactors will give us additional budget."

OBTW:

Practice the Art of the Possible, but do so without going through the entire alphabet.
- "I tried Plan A, but it didn't work."
- "I went to Plan B, but it didn't work."
- "I went to Plan C, but it didn't work."

Just like an emergency room doctor, sometimes you just have to look up at the clock on the wall and call it.

1.15 – TEMPERAMENT: THICK SKIN

Background:

Casting those who practice the Art of the Possible is incredibly important to healthy iteration. However, it does not free Teams from the pitfalls that come with strong personalities working the front end of a job and are under the pressure to quickly balance scope, schedule, and budget.

Sources of Drama:

- The ranks of the Artists, Designers, Operators, and PMs are filled with passionate people, and passion can be easily misinterpreted. When this results in someone going into the Team dog house or being the subject of behind the curtain chit chat, healthy iteration loses in several ways. The passionate one stops 'busting their butt' or holds back sharing helpful solutions out of fear it may worsen their standing.

- Additional downside arrives in the lack of trust between the various parties which drives waste, as doubts about the passionate one makes other Team members divide what that individual says by two, five, or ten. Also, the lubrication of human transactions – contact between people, is reduced.

Best Practices:

- Avoiding such drama is what Great Teams do through their leaders' default assumption that there are good intentions behind passion, and voting people off the island is not allowed to start. These Leaders don't reach for blunt instruments, nor do they even keep them around.

- The desire for diversity should not be limited to gender, religion, or race. In the case of projects, it should be employed in accepting a range of individual styles and passions. This is because Leaders and those that follow them have something very much in common – none of them are perfect.

- The desired end state is more than a group of people happy to work with each other on the next project. The best result is a group of people who see value in their colleagues, while the Project is underway, and do not want to waste anyone's time with personality detours.

- Effectively getting the oars of strong personalities in the water and in sync is a worthwhile effort because everyone's experience, skills, and dedication are needed. The task requires patience from Leaders and a flexible toolkit of approaches that are more art than science. For example, does the Team and the strong personality know who they work for? Left to itself, this question can result in a wedge answer, as personal allegiance ranges from the Artist to whoever signs my paycheck. Similar to WWII factory workers who believed they served those in uniform who used the stuff they built, the Team works to serve and exceed expectations of an Audience who will come to use and enjoy the Project. The Audience is the ultimate boss for everyone since no one wins "if you build it and they don't come."

- Artists in particular need thick skin, as their iterations are like a sculpture underway that keeps getting the fingers of others pressed into its wet clay. 'Fingers' may be cost driven, comments from their peers, functional needs, or equipment interfaces. Absorbing these injects successfully depends on the Artist moving to a place where they depend upon, expect, and may even look forward to others touching their work. Those that truly want to leverage the Team know they can't do everything themselves, and in fact don't want that burden.

OBTW:

The individual with the passion, has an obligation to temper it, as best they can.

On new Projects I frequently repeated the story of the 'cone of iteration' which I believed was one of the major contributors to a past Project's success. I was sharing that story at least once a week, until I accidently heard a hallway conversation among fellow Team members, "If I hear about the cone of iteration one more time, I'll scream." Oops, my bad.

1.16 – TEMPERAMENT: PAINT BRUSH SIZE

Background:

Question: "When will you make an end?"
Answer: "When I am finished."

This was the repeated question and answer exchanged between Pope Julius II and Michelangelo as he painted the Sistine Chapel ceiling in the movie, THE AGONY AND THE ECSTACY, which brought Irving Stone's book of the same name to the screen.

Sources of Drama:

- So, what happens if the Artist does not allow anyone else to hold the brush, or automatically rejects their work when they try?
    - In either case you have a schedule that is constrained by the output of a single talent, as opposed to work leveraged through many. When the other designers on a project are just there to move the scaffold, mix paints, or transfer design by pouncing charcoal onto wet fresco, everyone gets frustrated waiting for the one-man band to move to the next panel of the Sistine Chapel.
    - If the Artist insists on taking this route, others might take him up on it, but counter-propose that he just work faster. That is the equivalent of asking Michelangelo to use a roller or spray gun on the Sistine Chapel which will ultimately kill the Big Idea.
    - Unlike the Sistine Chapel where all the beauty flowed thru one hand holding a small brush, themed environments require the vision to flow through the hands of many, as it extends beyond a fresco to facades, interiors, sets, rides, media, landscaping, graphic, and dozens of other talents.

- *Just a reminder, we are not talking about the Artist needing to review all Creative work or take the lead on solving major issues. Those things are in the middle of their territorial interests.*

Best Practices:

- Pope Julius could not change Michelangelo's approach to work, and neither can you. To do otherwise would hold that person's artistic talent against them. That still does not overcome the fact that large thematic design efforts do not work well as commissioned works of art. The commerce (e.g., schedule) behind the Big Idea shrinks the places where the 'one hand, one brush' approach can be applied, and requires the Artist to be cast as an orchestra conductor rather than the third violin.
    - Again, the solution here is not lobbying Michelangelo to shift from paint brush to a paint roller or spray gun. Leave that idea at the door to the Sistine Chapel.
    - Instead, the approach is to help the Artist understand and embrace their orchestra conductor role, while clearly providing opportunities for them to pick up an instrument now and then.

Remember, you can't change the style that has made them successful. Success here is measured by the Artist's agreement to budget and seek design staff to assist them.

- On the other hand, if the Artist is deeply experienced, has been empowered to take the approach of one hand/one brush, and will not move from that strategy, you will need to:
    - <u>Not</u> default to, "This strategy is going to fail!"
        - The Artist, as a one-man-band, can actually be highly productive. After landing on the overall vision, some can have laser-like focus on how to execute it, and this can lead to them doing more and iterating less. The best of these individuals is highly prolific, which is a good thing.
    - Reasonably, stretch your schedule to accommodate the Artist's 'one-man band' approach.
    - Set interim goals with the Artist to see if they can reach specific deliverables milestones.
    - Understand how the Artist's vacation(s) will impact the Project.
    - Finally, if the schedule begins to slip due to inadequate output from the Artist, revisit the subject of leverage with them.
        - If they are not moved by the reality that they have become the pure critical path and need help, you may have to engage the Benefactor community to arbitrate an issue that has moved beyond your pay grade.

- The flip side of the coin is an Artist who routinely directs others in fleshing-out the Big Idea. If you have ever been blessed to work with this type of individual, you know that the Team of Designers working with the Artist will credit them as the creative engine, even though the Artist may never have drawn a thing.
    - However, don't fool yourself into believing the Artist who leverages uses significantly less time than a one-man-band Artist. That's because the Artist who leverages still needs to review the other's work, and they do not automatically accept the first, second, or even third pass at it. In fact, with more than one party involved, the work may iterate more than the one-man-band, and need an equivalent amount of time.

OBTW:

Homework for you - watch the AGONY AND THE ECSTACY and decide for yourself whether Pope Julius was a good or bad PM. The movie is well grounded in the tensions between Benefactors, PMs, the Artist, and the Big Idea.

1.17 – TEMPERAMENT: MOVING BEYOND TRANSMITTER AND RECEIVER

Background:

Moving into 'Team Mode' can be uncomfortable for the Artist, as they suddenly find themselves surrounded by new and old faces, each speaking the languages of their specialty, and all of them ready with good questions, as well as a few premature ones.

Some might tell the Artist to embrace the discomfort, but if healthy iteration and incorporation of Operator inputs is to start, there needs to be more than a transmitter/receiver relationship.

Sources of Drama:

-   In defense of a Big Idea (whose future requires a lot of things to go right) it is very easy for the Artist to represent it as an *immovable object* incapable of accepting change. Parallel to this, Architects, Engineers, and Operators are preparing their *irresistible force* of requirements. This formula of an immovable object meeting irresistible force lacks a predictable outcome, and Team members will begin to maneuver against each other.

-   Artists are not the only ones who can be prolific, and as others in the Team begin to flex their skills, they can easily produce a lot of 'too early' inputs that weaken or kill that which makes the Big Idea compelling. A sea of too early questions and/or requirements also kills its author's credibility with the Artist.

Best Practices:

-   The solution here goes back to picking your Team members well. While no one on the Team is there to avoid the tough subjects that come with their community's experience, early members are chosen precisely because of their ability to bring forward the most important inputs first, as well as distill them into alternatives that are less impactful and more complimentary to the Big Idea. The value of others from outside the Artist's community will be judged by how well they practice this.

-   Another reality is that Artists are prepared to change their design in order to progress it through their own community. For example, what was a single small-scale drawing will be developed into many larger scale ones, or storyboards, or models. These iterations provide a natural avenue for Designers and Operators to introduce and iterate their inputs simultaneously with the Artist's, albeit with their concurrence. The PM should endeavor to blend the Artist's natural progression of work with requirements brought forward by the Team.

OBTW:

Major inputs (e.g., asking for more square footage) are not gospel and have to be vetted by the Estimator and the Team before pencil or mouse is taken to them. There can be major cost implications that need to be challenged and confirmed before becoming actionable. Read the fine print of the Operator's input carefully, lest you commit to something prematurely.

On the other hand, if you need to exercise the input in drawing form to understand it better – let the Operator know that these are deliberate explorations of their propositions, and are not yet part of the design direction.

1.18 – TEMPERAMENT: PALACE INTRIGUE AND WATER COOLER DISCUSSIONS

Background:

At times the Artist and PM will be exposed to the ups and downs of debates concerning the Project within the Benefactor community and others above them.

Sources of Drama:

- A rollercoaster of rumors can derail a Team's focus, as people waste time guessing about what is going on. Like a pebble dropped in a pond, concentric rings of rumors pass from Benefactors to the Project Leaders to the entire Project Team, and then beyond the Team's limits.

- Rumors can encourage some key staff to jump ship, if they see greener pastures down the hall or down the street.

- The worst-case scenario from peeking too far behind the curtain is the Artist, PM, or both of them arriving at the conclusion that the Project will never be built. Even though they may not reveal this raw belief to the Team, their decisions will unconsciously reign in forward motion, as opposed to pushing the Team forward.

Best Practices:

- Yes, not every Project that gets vetted gets built. Many Big Ideas die on the boards. The Team should remember this is an underlying tenant of Project work, but it is something that should not be dwelled upon.

- Leaders are the greatest source of rumors for a Team. They constantly create rumors, as they speculate on upcoming Benefactor meetings, budget cuts, strategy changes, or design direction. This helps the Team maintain situational awareness. However, the potential escape of premature information has to be balanced with the Team's need to know what <u>might</u> be ahead of them. Emphasis on 'might.'

- Teams easily read their leaders body language and can sense when something is wrong or is going off the rails. While some things don't need to be shared, particularly if they are not material to advancing the design or are highly speculative, leaders should be prepared to answer questions even if the answer is, "I don't know." This includes rumors arriving on the Project's doorstep from outside the Team.

- If things have reached the point that the Artist and PM do not believe the Project will ever be built, only the Benefactors can restore the leaders' belief that the Project <u>has the potential</u> to go forward, and they should be engaged in a blunt discussion on the matter with their Latte Benefactor.

- Palace intrigue is not limited to mobilization and is something Project Leadership will need to keep in check throughout the Project's life.

OBTW:

"Never miss a chance...to keep your mouth shut." Robert Newton Peck

1.19 – TEMPERAMENT: FALLING IN LOVE

Background:

Definition of temperament: A person's customary manner of emotional response.

It is not unusual for art and architecture majors to fall in love with their first design, and stop further iteration. The good ones get over that.

PMs do not prepare drawings, fabricate show pieces, or place brick upon brick. Instead, the visible products of their work are strategies, schedules, and budgets. Like art and architecture majors, they too can fall in love with the things they author and refuse to entertain other approaches.

Sources of Drama:

- It is possible for PMs to fall in love with the first strategy they author. Committing too early or refusing to accept others suggestions may miss better opportunities, as well as signal the Team that their leader has trouble listening. If the PM forces adoption of strategies without healthy debate, they can end up as the sole owner of the strategy, particularly when things don't go as planned.

- A Project is not a democracy, but it is not a dictatorship either. This means that any shortfalls in the PM's skills as a facilitator, or stubbornness in accepting others ideas, will negatively drive the process involved with drafting and achieving consensus on go forward strategies.

Best Practices:

- Select PMs with strategic vision and who possess a temperament that does not lock down on strategies without considering others' input and consensus.

- Someone has to throw out the first stick, and it is okay for the PM to pitch strategies to the Team for their consideration. Also, it is okay for them to advocate for one, so long as they brief the Team on its pros and cons. This is the start of a discussion which will lead to frank feedback and consensus building.

- Welcome differences of opinions, and don't immediately attribute stubbornness to team members who say, "It's the way we have always done it." It may sound like their default answer, but perhaps they left something out. Perhaps they have tried the PM's proposal on previous projects, but after failing each time, they recovered by using their traditional approach. If this is the case, the PM has to figure out what, if anything, can be done to mitigate these very real and negative legacy outcomes.

- The Team also needs to remember that no strategy is perfect, and whatever is adopted may need to be adjusted down the road, as base assumptions fall short of realities encountered.

OBTW:

"If everybody is thinking alike, then somebody isn't thinking." General George S. Patton

1.20 – TEMPERAMENT: PERSONAL PRONOUNS

Background:

"Captain Sobel, you salute the rank, not the man." Major Dick Winters

While Dick Winters was actually a leader with tremendous informal powers, this scene from BAND OF BROTHERS had him employing formal power when an officer of lesser rank passed him and tried to get away without saluting.

Sources of Drama:

- Formal authority has a place, but it is the weakest authority a leader has to motivate their team.
    - Having people do something because of your formal title is the weakest reason for them to do it.
    - Leaders who depend on what it says on their business card to motivate the Team will find it works a few times, but not when you need them to pour on additional effort.

- In weak PMs, the use of formal authority is constant and can sometimes be accompanied by a visible pursuit of title and advancement. This is a toxic combination that a Team can't help but notice, and it will empty their bank account of respect for the PM. Emptying bank accounts is easier than filling them.

Best Practices:

- Informal authority is the strongest form of authority. It does not come from above; it has to be earned from those you lead by their catching you;
    - Being available and keeping your door open
    - Not avoiding difficult situations
    - Keeping a sense of humor, when times are tough for the Team
    - Promoting and developing others
    - Taking on risk
    - Sharing patience
    - Teaching
    - Taking the hits, and putting the shields up for the Team when it is the subject of criticism
    - Not engaging in name dropping
    - Not talking badly about others
    - Lifting others up when they are having a tough time
    - And most importantly, minimizing use of the personal pronouns 'I' and 'me.'

OBTW:

Keep the use of formal power under lock and chain. If and when it is ever used, it is the tool of last resort.

1.21 – EYE CANDY: RALLY AROUND THE FLAG

Background:

The critical artwork that moved the Big Idea to 'Project' status is the closest thing the Team has to a national flag, tribal symbol, or rally point. In the beginning, there may be a limited amount of it available to help others visualize the Big Idea, but what is available is gold to new talent.

While inspired words are good, they don't compare to a drop-dead gorgeous model or set of renderings. It is from these that those being on-boarded draw their initial brief, as well as inspiration. The best of these works naturally spur the human mind to fill-in details where none are drawn, and the more experienced the observer, the more undrawn details they will see.

When significant others, spouses, or kids are allowed to see the Project at open house events, it is not the schedule, strategy, or estimate that interests them the most. It is all about the eye candy.

Sources of Drama:

- The Artist may want to be sole person presenting the Big Idea's artwork to others, but they do not always have time to do so.

Best Practices:

- The Artist or their deputies should be the ones who do all major presentations of the Big Idea. However, as you move to the right on the schedule, frequent short notice meetings will be needed in front of model(s) and artwork, as Team members update their community on design direction or conduct problem solving with colleagues. To do this, they need to be grounded in the story and able to correctly read it back to others. Along these lines, it is nothing but a healthy sign if the Artist works directly with them to develop their ability to present the Big Idea for a limited range of audiences.
  - Words can accent, but can't compete with compelling ideas that are visualized well. To the extent that words are used to describe the Big Idea, brevity should be the goal. No amount of words can make up for weak artwork, but strong artwork can be self-explanatory with choice words serving as accents to what is already clear.

- Budget to freshen the Big Idea's artwork, because at the end of the phase the vision of the Big Idea needs to be more compelling than when it left Blue Sky. That's because there will no shortage of discovery that will temper it, as technical, functional, and commercial vetting results sit on the opposite side of the scale from the grand vision.

OBTW:

The deep integration of 3D modeling, as a deliverable, has definitely tempered the development of physical models. However, they still have their place, particularly when Benefactors want to sit around the Big Idea and speak among themselves without the Team there. At this stage, such a model does not need to fill the room, and the smaller size may lend itself to 3D-printing with a splash of paint to finish it.

1.22 – DESTINATIONS: DID SOMEONE BRING A MAP?

Background:

"If you don't know where you are going, any road will get you there." Lewis Carroll

This quote from Alice in Wonderland illustrates the simple pitfall that arises when moving out of mobilization without a short-term plan of deliberate next steps for the body of work to follow.

Sources of Drama:

The master schedule will still be in its infancy and chasing multiple critical paths, but a team without clarity on where it wants to be in 30, 60, or 90 days is in trouble.

Best Practices:

- To get things moving requires the Team's Leaders to collectively agree on the end state objectives for a specific period of time chosen (e.g., at the end of 90 days we will have…). Their focus should be on achieving consensus on the 'what' first, and work-out the 'how' later with the greater Team. The consensus on the 'what' can be captured in a simple and short FAQ that all understand and can easily recall or get their hands on.
    - o Example of FAQ to socialize with the Team for purposes of building a short-term schedule:
        - ▪ *What is the purpose of the funded effort?*
            - • *The Team is vetting the Big Idea's artistic, technical, and commercial viabilities.*
        - ▪ *What is the schedule for this effort?*
            - • *Work starts 1 June and ends with final presentation to Benefactors on 30 Sept.*
        - ▪ *How is the 120-day effort broken down?*
            - • *30 days from now*
                - o *Team is fully mobilized*
                - o *Job numbers are issued*
                - o *A detailed 120-day schedule is published*
                - o *A Design Review of the latest iteration of Big Idea will have been conducted (all Disciplines)*
            - • *60 days from now*
                - o *First pass at facility, show, and ride design and engineering strategies*
                - o *First pass at master schedule and estimate*
                - o *First round of cost and schedule mitigations*
                - o *Design Review of the latest iteration of the Big Idea (all Disciplines)*
            - • *90 days from now*
                - o *Second pass at facility, show, and ride design and engineering strategies*
                - o *Second pass at master schedule and estimate*
                - o *Second round of cost and schedule mitigations*
                - o *Final Design Review of the latest iteration of the Big Idea (all Disciplines)*
            - • *120 days from now*
                - o *Final design presentation materials complete*
                - o *Final facility, show, and ride assessments complete w/ mitigations made or proposed*

      o *Proposed next round of efforts priced and scheduled*

      o *Final report is completed and presented to Benefactors*

        ■ *Go/no go decision on next phase is made*

    ■ *What is the budget for the Project?*

      ● *Total budget is $85-million roughly distributed as follows:*

        o *$25-million for facility, utilities, and site (includes AE services)*

        o *$30-million for show (includes design and model soft costs)*

        o *$20-million for ride (includes engineering soft costs)*

        o *$10-million for general requirements*

    ■ *Who is the Leadership Team and when do they meet?*

      ● *Fred, Terri, John, Becky, and Jake.*

      ● *Weekly meeting, every Tuesday at 8:00am*

- Developing an actionable plan is the new team's first pass at scheduling and can be clunky or painful if not facilitated correctly. To be most effective, use whoever is the best listener and facilitator. If that individual is not your planner/scheduler, it's okay. The planner/scheduler still plays a key role in capturing flows and providing prompts.

- The body of the short-term schedule should also set timing expectations for handoffs between the Artist and the arriving design and engineering team members. What is known about the building, show, or ride may have been authored by the Artist up to this point. But now architects, theatrical designers, and engineers are on the scene and eager to take ownership of the next iterations. The timing of those baton passes needs to be synced and negotiated with the Artist's expectations.
  - o This is a delicate matter for the Artist. See <u>Stone Soup</u> in Part 2. It offers a technique that can be used to loosen the Artist's hands on the Big Idea so that others can start to contribute.

OBTW:

FAQs are one of my favorite tools, and they can be used for numerous problems covered in this book.

Rules of Thumb for your FAQs:
- Make sure it is a takeaway that you routinely keep to a page or less,
  - o You are breaking big and complex problems down into smaller ones.
  - o Team meeting agendas can be set up as an FAQ's questions, with the answers developed in the session.
- Make the questions important with emphasis on the What, Where, Who, When, and How?
  - o What are the long lead items?
  - o Where will the next review take place, the site or the Project Office?
  - o Who is responsible for securing a warehouse for the mockup?
  - o When does the building become available for our mockups?
  - o How do we plan to engage the Building Department on this issue?
- State the answers once and crisply.
  - o Do not say in three hundred words what you can say in thirty.

Finally, it should not go unnoticed that the entire Project is set up as an FAQ challenge by the Benefactors:
- How much will it cost?
- Can it open in four years?
- How much will it make?
- Where are the risks?

1.23 – DISCOVERY: GREENFIELD VS. LEGACY PROJECTS

Background:

Greenfield Projects are those developed on raw land.

Legacy Projects are those developed within the confines of existing Parks.

Sources of Drama:

- Sites that are decades old can be laced with uncharted and active utility lines, as well as abandoned ones that were never removed or located in documents.

- Touching old buildings invites an application of current building codes which can impact every trade.

Best Practices:
- Bolster your budget and schedule for researching existing conditions. Look at Legacy sites like an archeological dig.

- Address ADA (American with Disabilities Act) issues. This part of the code can be understood well this early in the Project.

- Be careful on the degree of change that you expect old buildings and facilities to accommodate. Know when you cross the tipping point that remodeling costs more than new construction. Bottom line – don't try to make older buildings do something they don't want to do.

- Make sure a first pass is made at gross demolition and abatement (aka: hot materials) scope.

- Understand the fragile nature of 'jumper cabling' live systems in a Theme Park and the catastrophic risk involved with working around Legacy systems. Examples:
  o A communications cable tie-in between legacy and new lines encounters problems, and all of a Park's point of sales registers go down.
  o A backhoe excavating for a tree accidently cuts through a legacy utility line that was undocumented.
  o Instead of abandoned water lines, live ones are found during demolition of old foundations, and an active part of the Park is flooded.

OBTW:

The level of surprise and discovery (which equals risk) in Legacy Projects can be much higher than Greenfield ones. Lower your expectations that everything will go smoothly in the field.

1.24 – TEAM INFRASTRUCTURE: NO ROOM AT THE INN

Background:

Like any new business (even temporary ones), you need physical space for work and collaboration.

Sources of Drama:

- This natural need would seemingly be easy to solve, but it is not. The facility manager for a company is used to PMs at their door begging for an immediate assignment of furnished space with conference rooms and network connectivity. However, it is rare that their response is, "No problem, here are the keys, and you have space XYZ for the next six months."

- Just like key staff are not sitting on a bench waiting for their next assignment, available office space and network backbone are usually fully committed. Thus, it is highly likely the Team will have to start out with a lot less than what they would want with many members, including key ones working remotely, and everyone fighting for conference room space.

- Yes, it is a healthy thing for your team members to walk a quarter mile to and from their office and the Team space. However, each trip could take fifteen minutes and you are paying for every one of them. Do it enough times during the course of the day and you could get up to an hour of labor tied down to movement between buildings. This is the kind of premium that can be paid for not being able to co-locate your Team.

Best Practices:
- The first day the PM is on the job is the first day this starts to get addressed. Otherwise, you will not even get the crumbs of what is available.

- The single most important area to bring online first is the 'Tribal Table.' For a Theme Park or Resort, this is the Master Planner's location. For a single attraction, this is the Architect's and Show Set Designer's layout area. Both are similar in terms of their large table capable of hosting several people around it. This is the Agoura or Town Square for the Project where transactions large and small are constantly taking place.

- Prioritize needs on conference rooms, network connectivity, the Artist's team space, and areas for hoteling.

- Occupy as soon as you can, so that the Team has a sense of identity.

OBTW:

Unless the space offered would embarrass your Team, don't be too proud to take what is available. If it is a temporary fix or solution, be aware that it will become a permanent one, if you do not keep pushing for better conditions.

1.25 – RULES OF ENGAGEMENT: "IS THAT A DRONE IN THE WINDOW?"

Background:

Sensitive projects and intellectual property create the need for rigorous veils of separation between members of the Team and those outside of it.

Sources of Drama:

- Fear is a lousy motivator, and each individual subject to security procedures knows that accidental release of IP can be a one-way ticket off the property. Fear creates hesitation and self-doubt. It slows things down and creates drag on transactions between people.

- Fear is compounded by human imperfection that presents the potential to leave something on a copier, forgetting to watermark, not shredding a document, leaving papers in a conference room, or a slip of the tongue on the lunch patio.

Best Practices:

- America is a litigious society, and many businesses just include this reality as a cost of business. Projects need to do the same.

- Given that it is unlikely that the Team will have much leeway on the procedures imposed, the best they can do is understand the impacts of these accommodations in terms of time and labor needed to enforce. Additionally, they have to clearly communicate these 'rules for the road,' and repeat them often as a necessary reminder.

- With so much information flowing, there will be accidents. Will Leadership speed dial HR for every infraction? Or, will they have measured responses to internal errors that did not result in a release to the public, and keep the issue one-on-one between a Leader and the person who made the error?
  - The answer is easy. Put yourself in the moccasins of the person making the error, and ask yourself which type of Leader would you want?

OBTW:

Unfortunately, as time progresses, the conditions and constrictions on the flow of information will only tighten. Today's rules will look easy to follow ten years down the road.

1.26 – CONTINGENCY: THE TEAM POT

Background:

No project plan is perfect, and imperfections can only be solved by one or more of the following:
- Re-strategize
- Re-prioritize
- Reduce deliverables and/or expectations
- Cut scope
- Add resources
- Add time to schedule
- Overtime and/or weekend work
- **Contingency draws** (the subject of this Chapter).

Just a reminder: 'pm' is used throughout this Chapter. It refers to the functional Leader of a community of professionals who are providing services to the Project.

Sources of Drama:

- If Project Teams are returning 100% of their budgeted contingency at the end of the phase, then one or more of the following occurred:
  - Budgets were bloated from the start.
  - Critical issues requiring more money and solutions were ignored.
  - A pm was afraid to ask for a draw on contingency because causation blame would be assigned to them.
  - Even though a contingency draw would have been the rationale solution, the PM made it extremely hard to tap. In turn, pumps stopped bringing the PM their problems, which means the problems didn't go away. Instead, they are now embedded land mines to be stepped on later.

Best Practices:

- Contingency is the Team POT. It is owned by the Team, and the PM manages it on their behalf. Team members should not be holding their own financial contingency pots.

- The PM needs to set common expectations on the management of contingency before efforts start. This needs to be done with everyone who is a candidate to contribute to or draw from contingency.

- Contingency is not the automatic first choice solution to a problem. However, it is there, with the intention to be spent, and the best leaders are not afraid to tap into it.

- The PM and pms should be constantly working to refill and add to the Team POT by sweeping unused funds (on completed efforts) or no longer needed funds (we only needed three mockups on that scene instead of five) into it.
    - If pms expect the PM to support them with contingency draws, they should expect to surrender budget back when they have underspent it, or no longer need it.
    - There should be healthy equilibrium in the push/pull between the PM and pms when it comes to contingency contributions or draws.

- It is not unexpected for contingency draws to become harder, as contingency and schedule are depleted. Accordingly, it is not unreasonable for a pm to consider some things may have been de-risked enough for this phase's purposes, and can be completed in the next phase instead of drawing on contingency to finish them in the current one.

- Team members should not expect that underspent moneys they turn into the Project are reserved for them or will be there for them to use later. Their contribution to contingency may end up as a draw by others outside their community, and it is not unreasonable to expect most disciplines to draw on and/or contribute to contingency during the course of a project. Bottom line - it is the Team POT.

- If the budgeted money for an effort is fully spent (or exceeded), but the effort is not complete:
    - A pm involved with a bust must evaluate progress across their community and determine if there are areas that will clearly underspend (not just hope to underspend). This should be done before seeking a draw of contingency from the PM. In doing so they are trying to solve the problem before presenting it.
        - This is more efficient than transferring the forecasted savings to contingency, immediately drawing it out to serve the bust, and dialing the causations into monthly reports to Benefactors who should be regularly monitoring the Project's use of contingency. Don't bother Benefactors with these types of happy endings, as they expect you should be doing them anyway.
    - If available money is spent, plus more is needed, and the same group has no clear and current sources of underspending – the PM has to act and draw on contingency. Other than an honest discussion on causation and any after the fact reporting of the bust, there isn't room here for debate on the need for the draw.
        - The only exception would be if the unfinished business lent itself to the next phase without unreasonable risk.

OBTW:

The PM's status report will categorize the purpose and causation of any contingency draw. It should not court favor nor be punitive in its reporting. Words chosen will either be reflective of a healthy relationship or drive a wedge into an existing one. Review your words with the pm associated with the draw, before you place that information in front of Benefactors. It is more than fair that you be accountable for what you say and put in writing about the performance of a pm and their community of professionals.

1.27 – AT THE END OF MOBILIZATION…

The Project has become a 'temporary business' that is now open for business with Benefactors moving to the sidelines as:

- The Benefactors' charter for the Team is clear and well understood.

- A critical mass of the Team's talent is in place and briefed.

- A short-term schedule informed by consensus on major strategies, deliverables, and milestones guides the way forward.

- Immediate roadblocks have been cleared, including where everyone is going to sit.

Expo Pavilion Concept

PART II - DISCOVERY

Part II will consume the bulk of the available funding. It starts with the mobilized team ramping up toward maximum output, as measured by the number of important decisions they make. Decisions will establish a foundational scope of buildable work accompanied by a business proposition.

In the end, what will look like a monolithic design is actually a collage of solutions from thousands of separate design problems. Some will be settled in a single pass, while others like a master plan could take dozens of iterations. The cliché of two steps forward and one back is a way of life here, as individual designs are developed, revisited, and then iterated back into forward motion.

The Team still lives the reality that no one knows how many design problems there are to solve or iterations needed to solve them. Leadership has made its best guess at the time, talent, and money required, but it is still a guess.

2.1 – MOMENTUM: START WALKING, NOT RUNNING

Background:

"Slow is smooth, smooth is fast." Special Operations Community

Sources of Drama:

- If you goose the Team to run all-out from the start with everything being a priority, you have no reserve to deal with the frequent visits of Mr. Murphy, who will demand attention and resources from what will already be an over-committed team.

Best Practices:

- Getting the Team in motion is like watching a little boy slowly walking along the sides of an above ground, circular pool. In the beginning, the water is slow to react. After the boy's second or third time around, the water is in motion. Come back five minutes later and the boy is being swept along in a current that seemingly drives itself. Water is a metaphor for problem solving and the little boy is the Team. Moving the water is equal to getting some wins under the Team's belt, and that success breeds other success.

- Ramping up a Team to maximum problem solving and output does not occur by accident. It depends on the Team having the discipline to know what their collective priorities should be at any point in time. They don't allow themselves to get lost in millions of decisions (the large body of water that needs to move), and focus on harvesting the prerequisites necessary for the next piece of work to start off efficiently, albeit not perfectly.

- Sprinting in the pool burns out the boy (i.e., the Team) before achieving the whirlpool effect. Like a marathon, the secret to success is finding a healthy pace the Team can sustain for the long term.

OBTW:

It is possible for a bad idea to gain momentum, until iteration reaches a point that its underlying weakness is revealed and the idea at hand replaced.

2.2 – MOMENTUM: NEWTON'S FIRST LAW

Background:

Back in the 60's, Captain Kangaroo's TV show had a yearly reading of STONE SOUP by Marcia Brown. It is the story of hungry soldiers returning to their country after war. Entering a village along the way, they seek food from townspeople who do not trust them. The soldiers are told there is no food, and they should keep moving. After seeing the same response throughout the village, they pause at its center and one soldier says aloud to another, "We should make stone soup." This piques the peoples' interest. Seeing that reaction, a soldier then says, "If only we had a large pot of boiling water." In response, a villager volunteers to provide it. Next, a soldier calls for three large round stones, and a man goes to gather them. One of the soldier's muses out loud, "Any soup needs salt and pepper." A woman runs to her house and returns with the seasonings. "A good stone soup should have cabbage," a soldier announces, and Marie goes to get the cabbages she had hidden earlier from the soldiers. You can see where this goes and, in the end, the soldiers and villagers all sit down to share a richly laden soup filled with all the things that had been hidden.

Sources of Drama:

- The front end of Newton's First Law is "An object at rest stays at rest." The beginning of STONE SOUP illustrates that this is an undesirable state.
    - The Villagers (aka: The Artist) do not yet trust the Soldiers (aka: new Team members) who have just shown up and are asking for food (aka: information). In fact, the Villagers (aka: The Artist) resist cooperation and may be hiding food (aka: design intentions).
        - Iteration locked away in the Artists' community and not shared, condemns Team members who have just arrived to a short life as observers, instead of contributors.

- If you see little use of the Tribal Table, your Project is stuck in 'object at rest' mode.

Best Practices:

- Although STONE SOUP starts with the raw trust problems a lot of Teams face, the balance of the story provides a model for the Project Manager and others to 'ignore resistance' in a way that gently probes the Big Idea and loosens fingers gripping it. The following example illustrates this.
    - Architect: "Well, the Blue Sky diagram does not show any catwalks, so I guess we don't have any?"
    - Artist: "Then how are we going to light the front of the stage?"
    - Architect at next meeting: "I've dropped in a catwalk here for the stage lighting."
    - Special Effects: "That won't work. You are blocking my laser."
    - Artist: "Oh, I forgot to tell you. We are cutting the laser, and want to use flame effects instead."
    - PM: (Realizing that this is the first time that scope has come up): "Real or fake flames?"
    - Etc....

- Applying the lessons of STONE SOUP can successfully lead to the desired back half of Newton's First Law, "An object in motion stays in motion." The thematic design equivalent to this is 'continuous, healthy, and prolific iteration.'

OBTW:

Some may think that this is an exercise in 'playing dumb' in terms of the questions posed (Reference the catwalk one above). All I know is that it helped me to get large projects moving, and it does not take long for what some would label dumb questions to begin to look like smart ones.

2.3 – MOMENTUM: HIDDEN PROBLEMS

Background:

It should be assumed that the Big Idea emerging from Blue Sky is full of hidden problems which threaten to make the Big Idea a bad idea.

Sources of Drama:

- Not catching a bad idea while it is still young, only increases it size.

- Bad ideas can gain serious momentum, when Teams step away from the truth by not admitting there is an elephant in the room.

- Killing bad ideas is perceived to be a third rail that one does not touch in fear of killing the Big Idea.

Best Practices:

- Good news: Bad ideas are just one or more iterations away from being killed.
    - Iteration is like the first olive out of the jar, once you get the first one out, the others follow quickly.
    - Increased frequency of iteration speeds up the discovery of embedded bad ideas.
        - Note: A project that reviews its progress work weekly or bi-weekly is moving faster than one that does it monthly.
    - Increased iteration also:
        - Keeps the elephant in front of the Team
        - Shakes-out pre-conceived ideas that were not fully informed during Blue Sky
        - Speeds up technical integration and accelerates the overall Project
        - Puts you that much closer to the final version of the Project.

OBTW

I have found that bi-weekly (say Monday morning and Thursday morning) design reviews are doable in the early phases of a project. Meetings are short, as there is not a lot of material to review, and you can still get a day or two for work to be advanced before the next session.

2.4 – SCOPE MANAGEMENT: WHAT DO MOST COUPLES FIGHT ABOUT?

Background:

The answer is MONEY, and similar to this conflict among couples, the latest ESTIMATE vs. BUDGET will be a constant and unwanted competitor for the Team's attention.

Sources of Drama:

- Day to day estimate busts are the norm for this business, and at times the Team may feel like they are in an endless game of "Estimate Bust Whack a Mole."
    - o "This week's trend estimate is over again."
    - o "We have to cut again?"
    - o "I can't believe it costs this much."
    - o "How could we have forgotten (fill in blank) in the original estimate?"
    - o "The last round of cuts was supposed to have taken care of this."
    - o "You're saying this bust does not include whatever is on the latest drawings?"
    - o "The historic numbers were wrong."

Best Practices:

- A synonym for the word estimate is 'Guess.' Estimates are a talented person's 'guesses' at what something will cost in the future. It may have no, little, or a lot of definition behind it.

- Pick your Estimator well. You need the truth and reality they provide.
    - o During the early life of a Project, the Estimator is probably the most important person assigned, after the Artist and PM.
    - o This is a thankless job in many ways, as the Estimator is a constant source of bad news to the Team. Not 'shooting that messenger' is the essential starting point to mitigating busts.
    - o The best estimators:
        - ▪ See scope that is not yet drawn or modeled
        - ▪ Provide venture estimate guidance for the Artist as they consider scope options
        - ▪ Don't put their thumbs on the scale just because more information becomes available
        - ▪ Point the Team toward where the money sits in the Project.

- Lastly, the Team is obliged to conduct an honest review of the estimate, meaning the Team needs to consider if any 'ups' in cost were missed, and not solely focus on 'down' opportunities.
    - o With review complete, iteration becomes the path out of the swamp.
        - ▪ Estimate busts are as much a design problem, as the look of a corbel. The path out is to de-risk the bust (reduce, eliminate, or otherwise make manageable) by iterating the design, strategies, or operations.

OBTW:

The PM should share estimate busts in private with the Artist, as opposed to reveal them as part of a Team session. This gives the Artist a chance to vent in private and the PM a chance to offer ideas on how the Team will be asked to mitigate the overage.

The Estimator and the Artist should be able to meet, as required, without the presence of the PM. This is important for the Artist's 'what if' exploration of design direction.

2.5 – SCOPE MANAGEMENT: WHEN IS CHANGE NOT A CHANGE?

Background:

Every iteration represents change, but not every change is a budget bust. In fact, the vast amount of change that emerges from healthy iteration should not be a bust. *The Author*

Sources of Drama:

- Iteration is perceived as an automatic budget buster.

Best Practices:

- When in doubt, the Estimator is brought in to act as referee.
    - o They are asked to judge whether an iteration represents an increase in cost or whether the scope that has evolved was expected and included in the Estimator's initial cost assessment.
    - o These conversations are rich with the Estimator's perceptions.
        - ▪ "The faux stonework's texture is well beyond what I assumed, but its square footage is less. I think you are okay."
        - ▪ Or, "You know, the textural images of that Greek hilltop village you showed me initially were simpler than what is appearing now. I think we have a problem."
- The Team needs to be accustomed to a steady stream of projected cost increases derived from the latest iterations, and cost mitigation pressures have to be shared by the entire team.
    - o Even though the drivers of the increase may come from iteration of the artistic vision, opportunities in building systems, back of house, contracting strategies, etc.... are evolving in parallel and deserve serious constraint lest they kill the Big Idea by their own weight and require an ever-larger piece of the limited budget pie.
- Teams cannot afford to succumb to "all cost mitigation, all the time." Again, the path out is the same as what got them into it – iteration. They must iterate their way out of the cost problem(s).
    - o Without this very deliberate iteration and exploring of possible solutions, wishful thinking can sneak in. This is usually manifested by setting under thought target cost reductions – "We'll assume we can do the mechanical systems for 30% less than the current budget." While the Team must retain an optimistic attitude toward the jam they are in, they cannot afford to fall back on hope as a solution to budget busts. Thus, they must iterate, iterate, iterate the Project's designs, strategies, and resource sources in search of more cost-effective solutions.

OBTW:

The PM should recognize that the Artist is going to push the envelope, and some of these raw design studies that have the potential to blow up scope can suddenly show up on the model shop floor or in a 3D visualization. That does not mean, however, that the Artist has decided to pull the trigger.

The PM and the Team can come across this 'doodling' by the Artist which may be just for the latter's internal consideration or to feed the Estimator some 'what ifs.' The PM should talk with the Artist to understand the potential for the new design to get traction, and share that with the Team so they understand the context of what they are seeing. No one should prematurely take it as actionable design direction until signaled to do so.

2.6 – SCOPE MANAGEMENT: ROCK STARS ARE NOT INFALIBLE

Background:

Being the birth parent of the Big Idea means the Artist is the ROCK STAR of the Team. This is not intended to infer black cape status on this individual, but instead it is to recognize that they are the FACE OF THE TEAM, the ENTREPRENEUR who got things rolling, and most importantly they serve as everyone's ultimate ONE STOP SHOPPING BELLY BUTTON for the Big Idea's design direction including any iterations impacting the look.

Serving as all things to all people on aesthetics and story puts the Artist on point for daily, weekly, and monthly approvals of design direction. Artists will be right most of the time, but what makes them GREAT is when they need to reverse themselves on a direction they have previously given, and don't let the Team get too far along before doing so.

Sources of Drama:

- To the extent that there is controversy here it is because one person's iteration can be another's painful scope change that fills conference rooms with angst:
    - "I've got breakage."
    - "We are throwing work away."
    - "I don't have time to go back and redo my work."
    - "We did what the Artist told us to do."
    - "Who is going to pay for the rework?"
    - "This new direction is going to take more hours than the original approach."
    - "How do we know the new design is going to stick?"

Best Practices:

- When the Artist introduces a change in direction, the Team should default to considering it a function of discovery and not error. Artists are just doing their job.
    - Discovery can't be predicted or scheduled. It is a natural process of thematic design.
- Great Teams never feel this as pain, as they don't see iteration as a license to endlessly change things. Instead, it is perceived as a path to a better solution, but not perfection.
    - The best Artists and Teams also understand they can't afford to iterate everything equally and have to place bets on where it is needed. An optimistic view of the outcome and a lack of fear of change is what makes the design iteration of Great Team's healthy.
- Budgets and schedules need to have some level of 'elbow room' to accommodate the Artist's need to revisit decisions made (as well as recover from failed mockups or technology demonstrations).
    - This is about 'right sizing' design durations, as opposed to the upfront deliberate scheduling of time to recover from decisions revisited.

- No one on the Team bats 500, and there will be 2 steps forward and 1 back at times, particularly when it comes to aesthetics. If your schedule and budget do not recognize this reality, it reduces the opportunity for healthy iteration.

OBTW:

Companies in this industry differentiate themselves by the degree to which they tolerate and can absorb the Artist changing direction.

2.7 – SCOPE MANAGEMENT: THIS IS NOT THE PROJECT THAT WAS PITCHED TO THE BENEFACTORS

Background:

There may be times when the Artist's eyes get bigger than their stomach, and the Big Idea gets so much bigger that the Team is unable to mitigate the associated cost increase.

And there are other times, when the Artist's vision evolves and what was sold to the Benefactors as the Big Idea, looks or performs significantly different. The Team then finds they have iterated themselves into a new Project.

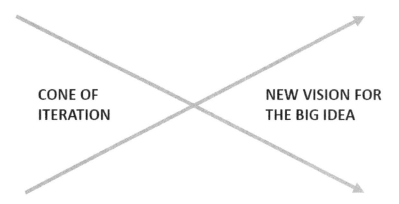

CONE OF ITERATION   **NEW VISION FOR THE BIG IDEA**

Sources of Drama:

- Both of the above are risky propositions, as there is no guarantee Benefactors will increase funding or approve the new direction. Getting a 'no' from the Benefactors may also come with blowback that can ding the Team's credibility.

Best Practices:

- The Benefactors always get the final vote on budget growth, as well as any major change in the direction of the vision.
    - The Artist and the PM need to be on the same page relative to the limited circumstances and number of times that they can 'go back to the trough.' That understanding should also be grounded in how easy or hard it is to quickly assemble the Benefactors to receive the new pitch.

- If the decision is to re-pitch, the Artist and PM need to decide what to do with the already mobilized talent:
    - Does the Team halt work on the original direction and everyone leans into the new direction?
    - Does the Team dilute itself and pursue both the old and new direction?

- If the Bigger Idea is rejected, time and cost were lost in its speculation. Similarly, if it is embraced by the Benefactors, time and cost were lost turning the ship in this new direction. It is important to recognize that these dollars and portions of the calendar probably need to be replaced, as the job restarts.
  o The re-pitch should include recovery cost and schedule implications.

OBTW:

Before getting on the Benefactor's calendar, use informal/progress work to pitch the Bigger Idea to the Latte Benefactor. Get their read on it, as well as recommended course of action.

2.8 – SCOPE MANAGEMENT: WHICH OF YOUR CHILDREN DO YOU LOVE MORE?

Background:

Unlike the equal love a parent has for each their children, the Artist and Operator can love one part of the Big Idea more than another.

Sources of Drama:

- Budget busts that continue to build without offsets can crush forward progress, as the Team becomes solely focused on estimate mitigation at the cost of artistic and technical iteration.

Best Practices:

- When all the cost trees have been shaken and there is no big money left to cut, the PM should call for the Project to be re-baselined. Ideally, this is a one-time event, such as prior to the Benefactor presentation, but it may have to come into play sooner.

- Even under the best iteration, some Teams will not be able to work the cost problem down completely. The Artist is then faced with touching the eye candy that got everyone excited about the Project. In addition, the Operator may have to defer some operational or maintenance capacity if the Project is to exist. Do they dilute the vision here and there, or do they surgically cut a discrete piece and leave the intensity of the Big Idea intact elsewhere? There is no easy answer to which of your children you love least, and this is a very private conversation Artists and Operators have within themselves and their communities. Solutions include:
  - The Estimator providing 'price tags' on the Artist's and Operator's 'kids' to assist in their decision making
  - Recognizing that only the Artist and Operator know which of their 'children' they are willing to give up
  - Accepting that the Artist is best positioned to know what the audience would most likely choose.

OBTW:

As a PM, I sometimes wondered whether the Artist deliberately added scope that they thought of as an expendable reserve to be cut down the line. The fact is that you will never know, so don't start with the assumption that such elbow room exists.

Note: some of these harder cuts can be put on an add-back list, if the estimate outcome changes or additional funds are found later.

2.9 – SCOPE MANAGEMENT: THE GAP

Background:

Until technology masters design in parallel with estimating, the two will continue to be out of sync, as design work moves faster than estimating.

Sources of Drama:

- Generally, the Team's progress work is usually:
    - days (if you are lucky)
    - Weeks (most likely)
    - Or months (not out of the question) ahead of the latest estimate.

- The above can result in the Team working hard and amassing potential breakage on something they can't afford.

Best Practices:

- Unless you have another element to put the Team onto, do not halt the Team's progression of design to let the estimate catch up.

- Do not let the gap between progress work and the running estimate grow beyond say two weeks.

- Make sure the Estimator has adequate resources to minimize the gap between pricing and progress.

OBTW:

Sometimes the scope will not have moved at all, but a major bust can come out of left field as commodity or union labor prices jump.

2.10 – TEMPERAMENT: HOW DO YOU SAY NO WITHOUT SAYING NO?

Background:

It is said that Eskimos have hundreds of ways to describe snow. PMs are similar in that they need many ways of clearly saying no without saying "No."

Sources of Drama:

- The PM has earned a reputation for saying "No."

- The PM's attempt to say "No" is so softened or diluted that it is a bigger "Maybe" than "No."

Best Practices:

- Just like the Artist sometimes employs 'No' in reviews of work underway, this answer is also available to the PM. However, just as the Artist may expand upon the negative response, the PM's reply should include the drivers of the 'No' with examples like:
    - "We could do that, but unfortunately the Benefactors said they don't want it."
    - "We could do that, but first we would have to go back for an additional $100,000."
    - "We could do that, but let's wait for now, until we see that Y has definitely happened."
    - "We could do that, but I want to wait for now, and save it for the next phase of work."

OBTW:

The "We could do that, but..." phrase above came from Don Edgren who was one of Walt Disney's key facility engineers. It was his response to my question, "Don, how did you ever say 'No' to Walt?"

2.11 – TEMPERAMENT: THE ARTIST'S CLAY AND THE KILN

Background:

When Walt Disney spent the weekend with Herbie Ryman at the Studio working on the first birds-eye view of what would become Disneyland, the resulting sketch was not really the final version of the Park. Yes, it had a path down Main Street with specific lands radiating off the Hub and a train around the perimeter. But when you take a closer look, it certainly isn't the Castle or other attractions in their final form. However, that sketch did its job by capturing the vision for the overall Park and established the nature of each land.

Sources of Drama:

- The Artist sees the Big Idea they have created as a culmination of passion, beauty, personal investment, and art that is still fragile and maturing. When the Artist feels pressured to produce answers for the Team, they may fear these answers will be considered final or permanent with no elbow room to change. Hesitation to share then arises in the Artist and angst emerges within the Team, as their source of design direction dries up.

Best Practices:

- First, recognize that the documents produced in this phase will not be used to permanently fabricate or build anything.
  - Bottom line - the Artist's clay is still wet and is not going to the kiln anytime soon. Construction and fab documents, which would start to and eventually lock down the Big Idea, are still a phase or two away.
  - Given that the final work of this phase will not equal the final design, the Artist is in essence reserving and outlining the specific scope for their vision.

OBTW

- As a PM, more than once, I advised Artists who were concerned about 'things going too fast' that the work currently on the boards was not the Project we would build. To demonstrate this, I would reference Walt's original sketch of Disneyland and describe how it took liberties similar to those found in the Artists current work.   I would also add that you had to 'squint' to see the real project.

2.12 – TEMPERAMENT: YELLING IS NOT A STRATEGY

Background:

No one ever knows how many decisions or human transactions will be required to answer the Benefactors' artistic, technical, and commercial questions. The PM and Project Leaders are charged with balancing this reality against a fixed amount of time by making casino-like bets (without the casino patron's risk of losing) on the Team's direction and progress every day. To do this, they have to keep a clear head so they can be more right than wrong.

Sources of Drama:

- The quickest path for the PM or a pm to burn-out is when they are the only ones on the Team losing sleep at night. Stress and drama definitely cross paths, but when that burden is carried by a few and not shared, things can become fragile and raw. This is the breeding ground of bad decision making, as governors on emotions are removed and relationships suffer.

Best Practices:

- PMs are not there to make sure their Team members avoid experiencing stress. In fact, one of their purposes is to distribute the sources of stress to the right parties, and ensure those parties own the issues.

- The majority of decisions and transactions between Team members needs to be made outside the direct participation and/or concurrence of the PM. The latter needs to trust others to constantly execute and exceptionally solicit help or feedback.
  - o The only guarantee here is that there will be times a Team member makes a decision that the PM would not have chosen. In these circumstances, a learning moment is not crushing the person. Instead, offer a light-handed piece of advice relative to 'next time.'

- Integration (e.g., I need this from so and so) is the most frequent area that the Team attempts to suck the PM into.
  - o Non-Critical Paths:
    - ▪ Although the PM facilitated the creation of the overall Master Schedule, pms <u>own all non-critical path integration</u> associated with it, and facilitate transactions between the requestor and source of input that include:
      - Negotiating the level of detail in the deliverable
      - The timing and milestones associated with the deliverable
      - Negotiating recovery plans if the deliverable is slipping
      - Confirmation that what was delivered was what was needed.
    - ▪ The PM needs to resist being drawn into non-critical path problem resolution. The pms are the ones who should be losing sleep over it.

- Exception: if any non-critical path recovery scheme requires release of schedule or budget contingency, the PM needs to concur.
  - o Critical Paths:
    - The PM demonstrates healthy integration behavior in front of their Project Leaders and the Team by facilitating the identification and negotiation of critical path commitments that cross multiple three or more professional communities. These are, "Do as I say, and as I do" moments. The PM shares ownership of these critical paths with the pms associated with them.
    - Ownership of critical paths that are within a single professional community or between two professional communities remain with their pms.
    - If a pm cannot get a non-critical path integration scheme back on track and it threatens to become a critical path, the PM is responsible for facilitating the development of a recovery path.

OBTW:

The PM's co-ownership of critical paths that cross multiple professional communities is a personal preference. That is because these critical paths can quickly become orphans, as the multiple hands involved can lead to oversight by committee which sometimes means no one is watching. Also, most pms will have multiple paths within their own communities that they are obliged to own and track, so it is not unexpected that the PM should have some too.

Lastly, Project Management could also be called Stress Management – a profession that deals with identification, distribution, and management of stress within the Team. This reality does not have to appeal to you, but the need to recognize that it is part of your job description is essential. Otherwise, don't be shy about stepping away from Project Management as a career path.

2.13 – TEMPERAMENT: "STOP ME, BEFORE I PLAN AGAIN!"

Background:

Several years ago, Imagineering provided an opportunity to take the Myers-Briggs Type Indicator. Out of the sixteen personality types, I pegged hard as an ENTP (Extroverted, iNtuitive, Thinking, Perceiving). I share that here of my free will and with no reservations.

ENTP strengths include:
- Quick thinking
- Excellent brainstorming
- Planning and developing systems
- Having a way with words
- Being energetic.

ENTPs include Walt Disney, Tom Hanks, and Thomas Edison.

If one is to accept the wonderful traits above, you also have to accept this personality's downsides, including:
- Being bored with day to day execution
- Losing interest as the initial excitement of an idea fades
- Being energetic can be interpreted, as being a pain in the butt, as opposed to being passionate
- Dismissing others or discounting their emotional points when debating concepts.

Caricature of Author as PM drawn by Artist during a Team meeting.

Sources of Drama:

- Myers Briggs test results are confidential information which takes it beyond a sensitive subject and into the realm of HR policies. Stay within approved lanes, and approach this third rail with great care.

- Even if such information is given freely by others, it can be mishandled or wrongly be used to manipulate them.

Best Practices:

- If one puts credence in Myers Briggs personality types, they can be useful in understanding strengths, as well as opportunities for improving transactions between people.
    - A certain personality type may prefer to receive a problem, close their door, study the issue, and return measured feedback. You should understand that you are probably not going to change their very deliberate style of problem solving, but that approach can be a strength by being a source of consistently high-quality work.
        - However, in time critical situations a strength can become a weakness. When exceptions arise and the Project cannot afford the time, help the deliberative personality understand (in advance) 'why' the Team needs them to expedite their decision-making process.
    - Appreciate peoples' strengths, and focus on helping them move beyond their weaknesses, as opposed to try and change their personality type.

- Unless someone very publicly volunteers their personality type with no reservation for use, (I elected to put my company plaque that declared me to be an ENTP on the wall of my office), focus on understanding and improving your own personality.

    - I enjoyed planning projects and developing process to overcome big problems. This reflected my Myers Briggs personality, and if left unto myself, I would probably just focus on that.
    - However, if I allowed planning and process to dominate who I was, I would have been a weak player – one locked into a bias to create rather than do. Knowing this, I made sure that my skills and reputation were rounded with being able to work through problems from solid hypothetical solution thru actual execution.

OBTW:

If a company goes to the trouble to provide you with your Myers-Briggs profile, it is for you to use in understanding your approach to work and potential areas for improvement. Otherwise, ignoring it is the same as an actor accepting the great reviews, but not heeding the critical ones.

2.14 – LEADERSHIP: CONGRATULATIONS! YOU ARE A REFRIGERATOR

Background:

Problems are just a magnet looking for a refrigerator.

Sources of Drama:

- Whether they like it or not, the Artist and Project Manager are refrigerators, and if there is not a daily stream of individuals in their offices attempting to place a refrigerator magnet on them (transfer a problem to them), then they are not leading the Team.

- PMs in particular are natural candidates to host lots of magnets with Team members constantly coming to them with:
    o "I don't have enough time."
    o "I don't have enough money."
    o "I don't have enough time and money."
    o "I am not getting the information I need."
    o "Paul is not getting along with Mary."
    o "We need more Team space."
    o "Our key vendor has too much work and just declined the job."
    o "I don't have the right people."
    o "All the plot dates are stacked atop each other."

- When Leaders shy from taking on problems that they should rightly address, the problems do not go away. They just fester until they cannot be ignored.

- Avoidance of problems can also lead Team members to believe it is borne out of their Leader's aversion to risk. It does not take long for Team members to see that magnets will never stick to aluminum refrigerators, and in their frustration, they easily share this new found knowledge with other members of the Team. Bad reputations are borne in this way.

Best Practices:

- At a minimum, leaders are obliged to listen to every problem that walks in their door, but that does not mean they can or need to solve each one. There will be problems:
    o The PM needs to take on because it is directly in their wheelhouse (e.g., Benefactor issues)
    o The PM instinctively wants to take on as they see it as a canary in the coal mine relative to a much larger problem
    o The PM lets ride to see if time makes them go away or confirms the need for PM involvement
    o Where the Project Manager reverses direction, and places the ownership magnet squarely on the one who brought the problem in the door.

OBTW:

Speaking of canaries in a coal mine. Ask yourself, is your door closed more than it is open? Teams observe the former more than you think, and they associate it with someone who is inaccessible <u>and not helpful</u>.

2.15 – LEADERSHIP: THE CARE AND FEEDING OF THE DESIGN PROFESSIONAL

Background:

"It is amazing what you can accomplish if you do not care who gets the credit." Harry Truman

Sources of Drama:

- Celebrating the Team traditionally takes the form of Friday beer bashes, pizza parties, or birthday celebrations. However, at the end of the day or the start of the following week, there is nothing to show for it, except for the remnants of the party in the fridge or trash cans. There might have been a speech or two that recognized someone for their efforts, but few will remember the words. These are momentarily good but shallow forms of appreciation. If not taken to a new level, they can become more about free food or taking a break instead of true recognition.

Best Practices:

- Work hard to catch your individual team members doing something that:
    - Solves a problem that has been dogging everyone
    - Clearly goes above the call of duty
    - Moves the ball in a new and usual way
    - Finds and fosters a new tool that advances many peoples' work.

- Recognition should be visible beyond the pizza party. Create a recognition device that the new 'hero for a day' gets to keep or hold until the next award. For example:
    - Recognition certificates with name, the accomplishment, team logo/graphic, and signatures of the Artist and Project Manager. The beauty of this is that you can award more than one, and they can display it at work or home. Individuals or groups are not restricted to how many they can receive.
    - Create a plaque or trophy that people's names are added to, and let them keep it in their office for a week.

OBTW:

The trophy approach can merge serious recognition with some humor. On one project I used a garage sale bowling trophy, and would add the winners' names to it every reporting cycle. There was actual competition among team members to see who would get 'The Bowling Trophy.' If more than one person receives this recognition, they pass it around among themselves, until the next recognition window.

2.16 – LEADERSHIP: GET OUT OF YOUR CHAIR, STEP UP TO THE BOARD, AND TEACH

Background:

"Give a man a fish, and you feed him for a day. Teach a man to fish, and you feed him for a lifetime." Chinese proverb.

Sources of Drama:

- There is no good reason for a PM to miss an opportunity to teach. The bad reasons include:
    - Equating information to power and not wanting to share power
    - Ignoring their obligation to mentor
    - Not making it a priority.

Best Practices:

- Teaching is one the most important "Do as I do" behaviors a Leader can employ.

- Additionally, like FAQs, a liquid chalkboard is a powerful thing, and experienced Leaders should never miss an opportunity to step up to it for purposes of sharing information or outlining their approach to a problem.

OBTW:

 One of my favorites 'Frank dropping me in the deep end of the pool' moments involved teaching.

It started with his calling me into his office and requesting a rough master schedule for Tokyo Disneyland. After providing some broad guidelines, he asked to see progress a few days later.

When I brought back the first pass, he studied it, and then sent me back to the warehouse to get three specific markers – Nile Green, Cadmium Orange, and Chromium Blue. Upon return, he took the markers and then started to highlight the portion of the master schedule that focused on Pirates of the Caribbean, and at the same time described aloud what he was doing:

- "Green will be facility, orange will be show, and blue will be ride."
- "The overall construction duration is close. Just pull it back two months, so we can fit in the landscape and paving time around the buildings.
- "Dash the green marker to indicate the landscape and paving duration."
- "There is not enough parallel work. You can start show and ride installation in parallel to the facility like this..."
- "And you dash the orange or blue to indicate test and adjust which follows solid lines for installation."
- "Leave several weeks at the end for operational training."

And before sending me off, he tested me:

- "If we use twenty months for the above ground construction duration on Pirates, how many would you use for the Castle? For Small World? For the entry Ticket Booths?"

This Master Planning 101 class took ten minutes, and at the end of it Frank had me back on track, productive, and tied to a format that would display the work crisply. While he certainly did review the final version, he never again had to pick up the markers on a master schedule.

2.17 – LEADERSHIP: KEEP THE MEDICINE CABINET LOCKED!

Background:

"Is that John Candy over there?" This is the question Joe Montana put to his team mates in a huddle, when they were down 16-13 with three minutes left in Super Bowl XXIII. It cracked the tension he saw in their faces, and the 49ers went on to win the game.

Sources of Drama:

- Pressure from above can sometimes force Team members to self-medicate, as a way out of tough situations. In their desperation, they reach into the Project medicine cabinet for COSTCO sized jars of:
    - Stupid Pills (aka: "I'll show them with this email!" – Hit send)
    - Hope pills (aka: "There is no way it can cost that much")
    - Elephant Pills (aka: "I don't see a large, grey creature in front of me").

Best Practices:

- Leaders are the primary source of pressure or <u>relief</u> for the Team. Look in the mirror and honestly assess (and address):
    - Whether you would want to work with or for you
    - Whether you let bad days get to you and walk around with a dark cloud visible to others
    - Whether you don't smile or laugh several times in the course of a day
    - Whether you have forgotten how to celebrate the good stuff that happens.

- If the situation permits, video yourself leading a Team meeting, and then watch yourself in action. If it is painful to watch, you have an opportunity for improvement.
    - Did you look uncomfortable?
    - Did you look stiff?
    - Did you ever smile?
    - How did you react to bad news?
    - Did you listen to others?
    - What body language were you giving those in the room?
    - What would you do differently next time?

- Bottom line - be the Leader you would want to lead you, and serve the others on the Team.

OBTW:

In addition to stress, just being tired can impact your decision making. Being a former architecture student who did many an all-nighter, I was particularly keen on one of Frank's pieces of advice, "Don't make any big decisions after midnight."

2.18 – LEADERSHIP: EYE ROLLING COMPLEXITY

Background:

Leaders can sometimes be so familiar with the information or concepts they present, that it is hard for them to fathom how others have difficulty seeing what they see.

Sources of Drama:

- Have you ever seen a Team's head spin, when the information presented overwhelms them with complexity or worse – it induces boredom?

- It is very easy to lose a Team's attention or focus, especially when you present information in volume or leave the outer shell of complexity around something that can be described in simpler, 'cut to the chase' terms. The following equations yield the same result, and are examples of presenting complexity, while masking a simpler purpose.
    - $(A + B)^2$
    - $(A + B) (A + B)$
    - $A^2 + 2AB + B^2$

Best Practices:

- Instead of starting with the raw equations, start with, "Did you know there are a number of ways to calculate the area of a square?"
    - All three of the equations above simply calculate <u>the area of a square</u>.
        - $(A + B)$ are two segments of a line that make up one side of a square.

- PMs dealing with complexity need to make it digestible for the Team, by breaking it down into a simple statement of the problem (e.g., How do you calculate the area of a square?), and separate any related, voluminous information into digestible buckets.
    - The military is filled with complex systems and tasks. They train the common soldier, sailor, or marine who is typically still in their teens by taking a task like land navigation (Did you know that the military uses three different norths?), and breaking it down into two dozen individual tasks of ten to fifteen minutes each. Each of these tasks builds upon the last one.

- Know and read your audience. Don't let their body language reach the, "You lost me," point.

- Leverage FAQs to brief Teams. Keep them to a page or less, and make sure it is in takeaway form.

OBTW:

Why say in a thousand words, what you can say in thirty?

2.19 – LEADERSHIP: BUYING A 2X4 MAKES ME AN AE EXPERT

Background:

A big dose of opinion here, but it is based on multiple observations from the point of view of a PM and Project Architect.

- Seemingly, many who have bought a 2x4 at Home Depot or built a playhouse for their kid believe it somehow makes them more knowledgeable about architecture and facility engineering than professionals in the field with decades of experience.
- What really makes this stand out is the significantly reduced tendency of PMs to pick at show and ride engineering decisions and strategies.

Sources of Drama:

- It is very easy to make AE staff feel like a commodity, when all they do seems to be questioned by the PM. Continuous challenging of their actions and decisions is easily perceived, as saying you don't trust their judgement. This can be a fast track path to lobotomizing your AE staff into "I don't care," or "Whatever you say," world. Just as bad is your scary smart people thinking, "Lots of other projects are around. I don't have to listen to this garbage."

Best Practices:

- If you want to be an architect or facility engineer, go get your license, and design some complicated stuff with it.
- If you want to be a partner, first try to learn why they did something, and then test that rationale (in your head) against what you were going to propose they consider. More often than not, their reasoning will trump your idea.

OBTW:

Being an architect, my unchecked tendencies were to be all over the Project Architect's work. This was the opposite of the Frank Stanek doctrine of avoiding telling someone 'what to do.' I learned to resist that temptation, and replaced it with leaving an impression of high expectations for the documents, and its achievement was dependent upon the architect's path of choosing, not mine. Those expectations were relative to both quality of the documents and efficient use of the Project's dollars.

2.20 – DESIGN PHILOSOPHY: TRIAL AND ERROR DESIGN

Background:

Design is not linear with only advancement. Steps backward are normal, and one of these can take the form of the Artist experiencing the equivalent of 'writer's block' with symptoms displayed taking the form of trial and error design.

Sources of Drama:

- When trial and error design become the 'go to tool' in the Artist's kit, this form of indecision compounds the already difficult forecasting of outcomes.

- It is not uncommon to hear members of a Team say, "Those facility guys are out ahead of everyone else again." The reality is that it is the Artist who has to be and remain ahead of everyone else. Unfortunately, chronic trial and error design will prevent that. Ignored, its frequency increases and progress will be similar to a plane without lift, as the Artist stalls in feeding direction to the Team.

- There is a limit to how long the design can wander, and the PM has to know where the point of no return is - the point where the lack of forward progress will require the Project to ask for more time and/or money.

- Trial and error design can be the symptom of a hidden problem churning within the Artist.

Best Practices:

- Diagnostics are in order here to flush out hidden problems by applying the following considerations and questions:
    - Does the Artist see this as an isolated situation or is more of the Big Idea at stake?
    - Is the Artist always locked into meetings instead of design sessions?
    - Is the Artist trying to solve too many problems at once, and if yes, can the critical ones be prioritized?
    - Has the Artist lost faith in the strength of the Big Idea?
    - Does the Artist feel that scope cuts or technical integration has killed the compelling nature of the Big Idea?
    - Does the Artist feel that they have nothing left that they can cut?
    - Does the Artist feel they need more help, or a different kind of help?
    - Does the Artist need some one-on-one time with their community's leadership?

- An alternative path to random trial and error might be to break some rules, or introducing some chaos to de-stabilize the status quo and see if the design rights itself.

OBTW:

Trial and error design is a legitimate tool, albeit an exceptional one that the Artist can employ to explore solutions. An Artist struggling with a concept should be given space to fall back on it, as a temporary crutch.

In some cases, the Artist can solve the problem at hand by leveraging a writer to tweak the story to eliminate a design element that is:
- Proving too hard to achieve
- Is no longer compelling in the evolving context of the Big Idea
- Or the new words clear a path to a better solution.

2.21 – DESIGN PHILOSOPHY: IS THERE A TIME TO FEAR ITERATION?

Answer: Yes, particularly when <u>chronic estimate bust recovery drives all iteration</u> and causes the Artist to lose faith in themselves or their design direction. The Artist is constantly forced to revisit things that were settled in their mind, and revisit them for reasons that are not artistically driven.

Sources of Drama:

- When each day brings another piece of the vision chiseled away with no end to this process in sight, it breeds false starts in the Artist's mind, "Why should I start designing (iterating) again? They will only want me to cut the things I just touched."

- If this negative attitude breaks-out beyond the Artist and into the body of the Team, doubt will breed doubt, and many will not want to advance work in fear that the iterations to get back to budget will consume the dollars and calendar reserved to advance the work. Suddenly, the entire value proposition is inverted and the purpose of the Project becomes mitigating an estimate, as opposed to defining an experience.

Best Practices:

- Generally, Benefactors are not going to give you relief on this. They expect the Team to get back to budget.

- Just like a kidney stone feels as though it will never go away, it will, and so will the pain of mitigating estimate busts.

- Project Teams that find themselves stuck in a repeated Ground Hog Day of major estimate mitigation, need the PM to perform the forensics which will reveal one or more of the sources below as causation.
    - The original rough order of magnitude estimate was really off
    - The scope has and is growing unchecked
    - The technology is too bleeding edge
    - The current estimate trend is incorrect
    - There is too much time in the Project
    - There is too little time (inefficient compression) in the Project
    - There are 'downs' that are not being included.

- Once causation is found, it will still take an all hands effort to reduce the problem from the death of a thousand cuts to a one-time dose of bitter medicine. The PM should move the Team toward a major reset that addresses the causation and total bust.
    - Assuming the total bust is overcome, the Team can get back on the road to iteration associated with advancing the design.
    - If they are unable to recover to budget, it is time to sit down with the Latte Benefactor.

OBTW:

An additional form of iteration to be concerned about emerges from Teams who know they will be on the Project for years and are thinking, "I'm designing today, tomorrow, next month, next year, etc...."

This complacency breeds revisiting ideas that were well settled with questions like, "Do we still have time to...?" Unchecked breakage of work previously done, and done well, is the end state here.

2.22 – DESIGN PHILOSOPHY – BLANK SHEETS OF PAPER

Background:

Although it sounds like a deep dive in creativity, starting with a blank sheet of paper is similar to starting a building without a foundation.

Sources of Drama:

- Individuals who need to start everything with a blank sheet of paper will likely take more time than someone who does not bypass legacy knowledge.

- One of the worst outcomes is that creating everything from scratch can lead to solutions which are less compelling, functional, or robust than those designs that have learned from or leveraged existing designs.

Best Practices:

- There is nothing wrong with standing on those who came before you. They are there to build upon.

- Reserve blank sheets of paper for hero moments in a design that make it unique and inspired.

OBTW:

Estimators do this naturally, particularly during the early phases, as they seek similar legacy Projects that can be adjusted and brought forward in time, as a basis of comparison and/or surrogate for the Big Idea's cost.

2.23 – INSTINCTS: THE 'VOICE'

Background:

There is usually a good reason why you are getting, 'that old sinking feeling."

The phase following Blue Sky is not very long, and the time you have available to react to major shortfalls in its progress is similarly short.

Sources of Drama:

- Ignoring your gut (aka: The Voice) saying the Project is falling short on key results, and running that situation to failure leaves you showing up in front of the Benefactors with a request for more time and money instead of answers.

Best Practices:

- Listen to your gut (aka: The Voice). But, do challenge it and ground it with the things that have not happened, but should have.

- If the Voice is solidly saying you need more time and/or money to complete the phase, you need to share the evidence with your Latte Benefactor and get their advice.
    - o Taking your lumps early may allow you to keep your request to just additional funds and accomplish the recovery work within the approved timeframe.
    - o Waiting until the back half of the phase to make the call defaults you into needing both time and money, and time always seems to be harder to get than money.

OBTW:

Requesting more time or money from the Benefactors is nothing less than a very exceptional event. Be assured, there is a limit to how many times you get to go back to that well.

2.24 – INFORMAL POWER: CHECK YOUR CREDIT SCORE

Background:

"Sometimes Sir, the troops need to know that you were behind the good thing that happened to them."
Platoon Sergeant giving advice to the Platoon Leader (Author).

Sources of Drama:

- A good leader routinely does things for the Team that they never see them do. And a good leader does not routinely beat their breast saying, "Look at what I have done for you." Unfortunately, if all the Leader's good actions are hidden from view, the Team's impression of them could be well short of reality.

Best Practices:

- It is okay to let the Team occasionally catch you doing something on their behalf.
    - Just make sure that you acknowledge with a simple nod of the head, and not a sweeping, end of the Act 4 bow.

OBTW:

Advice to the PM from the Team is free. It best flows when breaking bread in a small group or from one-on-one sessions. And if you adopt that advice in some shape or form, make sure its author gets the credit.

2.25 – INFORMAL POWER: IT WAS A GOOD IDEA, UNTIL IT WASN'T

Background:

You need everyone on your Team taking initiative whenever and wherever they can.

Sources of Drama:

- The downside of initiative is error, and when error is addressed with inquisition or punishment, risk aversion replaces initiative, as the Team comes to believe the PM does not have their 'Six.' Punishment wrapped in risk aversion is the quickest way to lose informal power.

Best Practices:

- Part of a PM's job is to unlock a Team's initiative, encourage them to take risk, and not punish them for failed initiative. But to do this, the PM has to have the mental athleticism to tolerate errors and failures that occur pretty regularly. How the PM handles initiative failures will either empty or make a deposit in a Team member's bank account of faith in the PM as a fair leader.

- Sometimes you have to give the risk averse one something in writing. Several times I took one of my business cards, turned it over, labelled it as a GET OUT OF JAIL FREE card and signed it. I then gave it to someone who wanted proof that they would not get slammed if they failed to achieve the stretch goal, I was asking them to pursue. Out of dozens passed out over the years, the one below was the only one ever turned in. I asked the individual why they felt they had to use it. His response was, "I don't need it anymore."

OBTW:

One of my favorite moments as a Design Manager (pm) involved a budget bust.

Sensing a theater was about to go under significant iteration, I gathered the engineering team and said, "We should hold on advancing work further because there is high probability the next iteration is going to have a major impact on building systems."

That impactful iteration did occur, and three weeks later one of the engineers was in my office apologizing, "I know you told us to hold, but I was so close to finishing and I was about to lose my draftsman to another project. So, I went ahead and spent the rest of my funds and completed the work. Based on the new design direction, I have breakage now, no money, and need 200 hours to redo the work."

I looked at him and said, "This is what I just heard. I thought there was a chance the iteration would not occur or affect me, and if I lost my draftsman, it would have impacted my ability to support the upcoming milestone plot. I took a chance, and finished the design."

He nodded and I ended with, "We don't punish initiative on this Project. Thanks for making a bet you thought would have helped. I make bets all day long, and sometimes I am very wrong. Spend the 200 hours you need. It will go down as extended iteration and not an error on your part."

From that day thru the end of my career at Imagineering, this engineer and I had a shorthand of trust that positively impacted negotiating estimates of services, schedule durations, and general problem solving. If he said that was the best number he could do, that was the best number he could do. If I proposed a new delivery strategy, he was willing to take the chance, and he would do all he could to make it work.

2.26 – INTEGRATION: PARALLEL WORK FLOWS

Background:

The NATURAL SEQUENCE OF FIELD WORK typically has construction (e.g., deep utilities) starting ahead of show and ride fabrication. This example is just one of many that feed a Project's parallel work flows.

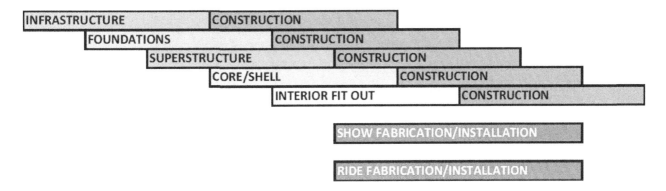

Sources of Drama:

- In the old days, when dinosaurs roamed the land, work was more linear. Today, parallel work flows are the norm. This pressures the Team to focus on information drawn from immature portions of the design which in turn puts tremendous pressure on the Artist.

Best Practices:

- The PM has to ensure that the Team understands the implications of parallel work. It is not going away, and will increase dramatically, if the Project is greenlit to move forward.

- Some good news here. The artistic and technical integrative work following Blue Sky requires the least amount of information, as compared to the phases that follow. The Team is typically not dealing with large quantities of bread box size equipment, and the terms gross and rough are the operative adjectives in describing the level of inputs needed.
    - However, this is the time to exercise the Team's integrative muscles. In this phase, they have the least amount of information to harvest and integrate. Thus, this is the ideal time to establish and exercise work flows between the different professional communities.

OBTW:

Led by the PM, the Team needs to learn how to do Pull Planning in this phase, as it has the fewest activities to integrate, and the least number of players in the room, as compared to downstream phases.

2.27 – INTEGRATION: ZOOM OUT TO SEE THE PROBLEM AND SOLUTION

Background:

The reality is that the technical information needed in this phase is a small subset (see yellow area below) of all the information that will ever be produced for a facility, show, or ride element.

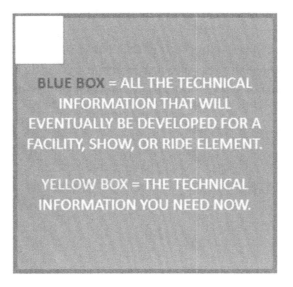

Sources of Drama:

- Drama arises, because even though the facility input needed is a small fraction of what will eventually be developed, the timing of its availability is out of sync with the natural flow of its development.

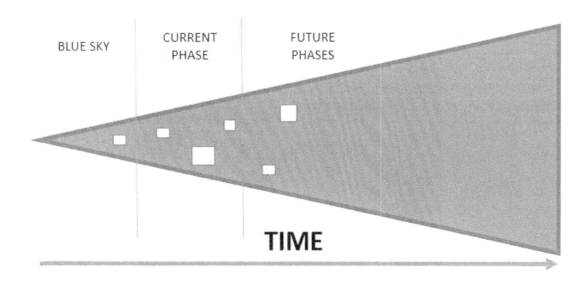

Best Practices:

- First, recognize that all disciplines are not working at the same level of detail, and in fact they will never be in perfect sync with each other. Someone will always be pushing or pulling information from another.

- Second, do not underestimate the need to clearly state the <u>minimum</u> 'ask.' Leaders should leverage FAQs to describe what is needed, why it is needed, and when it is needed.

- Third, you do not need everything at once. The facility build is spread out, and therefore the inputs needed by architects and engineers can also be spread out by placing them in separate 'WAVES' of information. Prioritize what you need, and only ask for what you need.

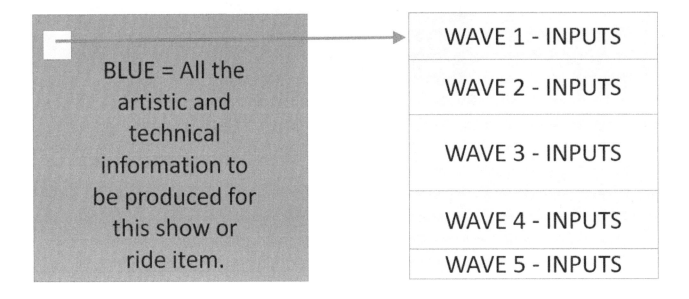

BLUE = All the artistic and technical information to be produced for this show or ride item.

WAVE 1 - INPUTS
WAVE 2 - INPUTS
WAVE 3 - INPUTS
WAVE 4 - INPUTS
WAVE 5 - INPUTS

OBTW:

Your integration work flows need to include closing the loop. The PM should remind the Team to avoid the pitfalls that arise when you run with someone's information, and never show them what you did with it. No one can afford to be just a puller or pusher of information – they need to be both.

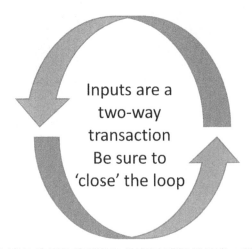

Inputs are a two-way transaction Be sure to 'close' the loop

2.28 – INTEGRATION: "DON'T YOU GUYS TALK?"

Background:

Integration is the lifeblood of any project. Information must freely flow between artists, designers, technicians, architects, engineers, and operators. This takes the form of artistic and technical exchanges with commitments made between as few as two, or as many as a dozen or more people.

To the extent that there are successes, these are usually found within each professional community – Artist talking with writer, ride track engineers talking with ride control engineers, or architects talking with facility engineers.

Sources of Drama:

- Integration requires people to leave their cube, go to another near or far, and negotiate information exchanges. This sounds very simple, but in fact, it does not occur automatically or naturally, particularly when the transactions cross professional communities.

- Integration is probably the most significant source of drama and stress for the Team outside of balancing estimate and budget. Even a single request, "This is what I need," can unleash a series of questions and statements along the following lines:
    - Why do you need it?
    - Why are the Architects and Engineers ahead of everyone else?
    - When do you **really** need it?
    - I haven't even figured out what mockups need to be done.
    - The Artist is still thinking about this part of the show. It could change big time.
    - When do you **really, really**, need it?
    - If I give you something, it is going to be wrong.
    - I need X from so and so, before I can give you Y.
    - When do you **really, really, really** need it?

Best Practices:

- First, start with the mindset that you are not looking for perfection this early in the Project.
    - Gross input can be good input, if it has the elbow room to accommodate a rationale amount of growth and adjustment.

- Second, instead of the Artist experiencing a death of a thousand cuts by being bombarded with requests for information, put the Artist in a work session with the twenty plus people who are the requestors and sources of technical information. The Artist's guess is always better than anyone else's, and as the design progresses, you may need additional sessions. One on one and smaller group sessions will spill out of the major sit down, and be more effective thanks to it.

- Third, and last among preferred choices is a Team member making a guess in the absence of the Artist or others being able to respond.
  - Example: Everyone agrees a pit will be needed to hide the base of a large animated figure, but information on the figure is practically nil. The Artist gives a range of possible sizes, but in response the Animation reps say they have no idea what the pit should be. The Architect speaks up, "Does anyone have a problem if I show a 6'x6'x6' pit here so that the Estimator reserves some budget for it?"

In the above example, doing something is better than doing nothing, and the pit will be visible on the documents or 3D model as a constant reminder of unfinished business.

OBTW:

I have been blessed to have repeatedly worked with incredible show equipment designers over the years. However, despite the repetitive nature of our engagement, many times the conversation from the other side of the table started with, "What is it you need?"

Yours truly would bite my tongue, accept that I was Bill Murray in a Groundhog Day moment, and offer the reply that I had given a dozen times before, "Locations and rough dimensions for equipment bigger than a Prius, plus rough access requirements, and gross weight for suspended objects above 2 KIP. Eventually, I captured the Groundhog Day elements and put them into an FAQ.

Lesson learned: Take nothing for granted and apply patience in large quantities.

2.29 – CONTINGENCY: MAKING STUFF BIGGER

Background:

Technical contingency is adding more 'stuff' to a design, as opposed to carrying financial contingency.

The less that is clear about the physical scope of the Big Idea, the more risk grows that the current design will not be able to accommodate the final design. Such risk is typically offset by applying technical contingency (e.g., that which goes beyond code). Examples:
- Engineers increase beam size for unknown loads that may evolve in the design
- Architects increase interstitial space so wall types can be adjusted without violating a zero-lot line
- Ride engineers round-up forecasted vehicle weight, when the level vehicle decoration is still very conceptual.

Sources of Drama:

- It is easy for inexperienced internal or consulting staff to miss areas that need technical contingency, or apply an amount that is grossly beyond what is needed.

- No one likes to be wrong, and the danger with applying technical contingency is that some Project Team members may have received memorable blowback on past projects for downstream cost increases arising from not giving themselves enough elbow room early in a project. Such experience is valuable, but if the muscle memory of that past is painful, fear can cause too much thumb to be put on the technical contingency scale.

- Hope is not the same as optimism, and it is a lousy strategy, as it can blind decision makers. Example:
    o In a team meeting the Structural Engineer tells the Architect, "I need the locations of suspended catwalks to size roof members."
    o The Artist, desperate to cut costs somewhere other than the show, hears the question, and responds, "Absolutely, no show equipment is suspended from or placed in the ceiling."
    o This is contrary to both the Architect's and Structural Engineer's deep experience on similar projects. Drama comes in when they wrestle with their gut feeling and the Artist' desires.

Best Practices:

- There is no getting around it - technical contingencies can directly drive costs up. However, ignoring them leaves the Team with no flexibility downstream, which can be a direct path to catastrophic technical or financial failure. Just as the Estimator is pricing what is not yet visible, Project Leaders should expect designers and engineers to be doing the same in their application of technical contingencies.

- Not every aspect of the design requires technical contingency. It should be applied exceptionally.

- Understand that, when it is applied, there is no guarantee it will be able to handle all design evolution or discovery. At least though, you are starting with something instead of nothing.

- To the greatest extent possible, lean on senior technical staff to suggest technical contingencies for discrete risks.

OBTW:

Not every up-sizing survives contact with the final estimate. There can be 'downs,' as some risks will not materialize over time. Team members must ensure technical contingencies are removed, when it is clear they are no longer needed (e.g., the ride vehicle ornamentation becomes simpler than originally thought), and the Estimator needs to be aware of this de-scoping

2.30 – CONTINGENCY: DEATH BY ROUNDING-UP

Background:

"A good estimate for professional services is within +/- 5% of actual costs." The Author's personal rule of thumb.

As a Design Manager, I would share this point of view with departments during solicitation and negotiation of their estimates to remove fear from their pricing.

As a Project Manager, I would also share this point of view with functional areas and add that if their work did go over by up to 5%, I would not assign causation as an error on their part. I did this to reduce their feeling the need to round-up out of fear of public shame during month end reporting. Without disarming their fear, they might have hidden contingency in the body of their work, which would have been on top of the contingency I carried.

Again, none of this was institutionalized. Like the other content of this book, where guidance was not provided, a PM has to innovate.

Sources of Drama:

- Everyone's pricing will be wrong, and they know it. That is, actual costs for professional services will not land perfectly within the exact dollars allocated. These educated guesses are typically done in a short amount of time against an even shorter amount of information, and have to consider such things as:
    - How productive will the Team be in design?
    - Will everyone be able to start as planned?
    - How many pieces of information will be received late?
    - How much real breakage will occur as the design iterates?
    - What will the final mix of labor rates be vs. the assumed rates?
    - How many of my staff are new to the software?
    - Will key mockups be successful or struggle as proofs of concept?
    - How much new technology may change the design or engineering direction?
    - How busy will the industry be when work is bid to consultants, vendors, or contractors?

- Caveats to estimates are good, but if you do not remove fear from those pricing work, it is easy to end up with them writing more about what they are not going to do, as opposed to what they are planning on doing.

- Fear is not the same, as prudently tackling a Project's risks and considering what can be done to mitigate them. Negotiating without listening is the mother of hidden contingency.

- Team Member: "I think we have a chance to land on a master plan in ten iterations, but there is no way to really know. I am going to price ten, but I want to make sure you are carrying contingency, if <u>we as a Team</u> can't reach consensus in ten."
  - Project Manager: "We'll cross that bridge when we get there."
  - Team Member: "You are going to carry something, right?"
  - Project Manager: "You'll run out of schedule before you run out of money. Again, we will cross that bridge when we get there. Just sharpen your pencil and give me your best number."
  - Team Member: Reflecting about the meeting just ended, *'The PM didn't listen. I am going to goose the hours for each of the iterations.'*
  - Project Manager: Reflecting on the meeting and privately speaking to the Estimator later that day, "Let's make sure our contingency can accommodate an additional week of iteration."

- Past history with people can also breed hidden contingency.
  - The scenario above gets even worse, if the Team Member has had a bad experience working with the PM: *'Yeah, he released contingency last time, but assigned causation to my department as an estimate bust, instead of flagging that the Team could not agree on a master plan. I'll price work to make sure that does not happen again.'*

Best Practices:

- Contingency is intended to be spent, but spent judiciously.

- Contingency amounts should be recommended by the Estimator and validated by PM and pms.

- Team members should estimate their work, but not add a contingency to it.
  - Instead, they should price a rationale path for their work with key assumptions caveating the outcome. These caveats and their risks should clearly be cited and discussed with PM.
    - Many of these caveats will influence the overall contingency applied.
  - The price for Team members not applying their own contingencies is that Project Leadership cannot ignore the risks they identify.

- To the greatest extent possible, lean on senior staff to suggest where contingency is needed for discrete risks. Less experienced staff may not grasp risk consequences or go significantly beyond what was needed.

- Similar to technical contingency, not every allocation survives contact with the actual costs. There can be 'downs,' as risks fail to appear. Make sure these downs make it to the Estimator, as they are encountered, as opposed to saving them for the final report.

OBTW:

Taking AE services, as an example, I found the more that I broke down discrete tasks, the more I had to round all of them <u>down</u>. Rounding up would have otherwise had a compound interest-like impact – the classic death by hidden contingency would have resulted.

2.31 – AT THE END OF THE MAIN BODY OF WORK...

To get here, the PM and Artist believe they have reached critical mass, and are ready to bundle their findings into the final Benefactor presentation.

Most of the allotted time and money have been spent on a path that was anything but straight with progress now needing to be coaxed and wrangled into a succinct story that will either kill the Project or let it live another day.

This is the moment the Benefactors hold the PM accountable for forecasting outcomes. However, the PM's grade on predictability is not based on the Team guaranteeing the Project meets all the conditions to make it viable. Instead, the measure of the PM is made against their ability to know that conclusions are sufficiently reliable (whether good or bad outcomes result) for the Benefactor's to render a Nero-like verdict (thumbs up or down). This is similar to a sailor holding paddles on the back of an aircraft carrier. As a plane (the Team) approaches for landing, that sailor (the PM) will either be satisfied, or wave them off to take another pass.

Diorama Scene 3 – War in the Pacific

PART 3 - ARE WE THERE YET?

To get to this point, the PM has concluded that the Team has produced all the answers needed by the Benefactors who are generally looking for a summary that leads to a binary answer.

- We can make this Project work,
- Or we can't make this Project work.

If the Project is found to be doable, any 'add-ons' should be placed on a buffet table of options to be presented in the presentation. These are items that are not necessary to make the Project work technically or financially, but represent additional opportunity (e.g., going to a larger vehicle for ride capacity).

If the Team cannot make the Project work without a lot of things having to going right, they should still provide that circuitous path salted with the risk they have found, "This Project could work, if we assume the following…" It is then up to the Benefactors to judge whether the caveats are within their tolerance levels.

- The more that success follows a twisted path of things that have to go right, the more ammunition you have given the Benefactors to kill the Big Idea. Under these circumstances, it probably will not take long for the Team to get a go/no go answer.
- Fewer risk caveats yield a different kind of reflection on the part of the Benefactors. The potential for success actually slows them down as they ponder whether they really, really, really want to do the Project, or at a minimum fund the next phase of effort to avoid lost opportunity.

3.1 – MOMENTUM: IT'S ALL IN THE COMPUTER (MAYBE NOT)

Background:

Computer-based 3D modeling has reduced the amount of physical modeling required to advance a Project, particularly because it is a faster source of visualization than hand-cutting matt board. While the computer has not replaced the sculptor's hand in rockwork or other organic shapes, it has put significant pressure on the need to physically model for study or final presentation purposes.

Sources of Drama:

- In a Team space filled with computer-based 3D modeling, some PM's instincts discount the need for physical models. The associated problems with this approach arise from:
    - o Computer-based 3D modeling allowing endless editing. While this is good for basic iteration, if left unchecked, it deprives a Team from seeing the need to arrive at a natural end state the way completing a physical model does.
    - o Allowing primary iteration (via 3D modeling) to continue all the way up to the final Benefactor meeting leaves no time for the Estimator or others to finalize the meeting's deliverables.

Best Practices:

- Establish a milestone that reads, 'Final input to model builders.'
    - o Adopting a physical model, as a deliverable for the final Benefactor's presentation, forces the Artist to bring things to closure ahead of the meeting in order to build the model.
        - It is not out of the question that computer-based 3D modeling is the primary form of iteration, up to the point that the Artist feels they have achieved the critical mass and configuration needed to build a model for the Benefactor presentation. From this point, multiple and parallel efforts flow and:
            - A traditional physical model is started or the final one printed
            - The Estimator begins their final push on the numbers for the Benefactor presentation.
        - Yes, the Artist working with the model makers will be 'slamming things in' like color, trees, people, and props, as the presentation date approaches. But all of these are just dressing over a critical mass and configuration that were achieved earlier – and are holding.

OBTW:

- Unlike a 3D program, no special skills are necessary for a Benefactor or anyone else to 'fly themselves' through a physical model.

    - o Example: Benefactors are able to meet around the model without the Team in the room.

3.2 – MOMENTUM: PENCILS DOWN

Background:

As the Team approaches the Benefactor presentation, some form of 'pencils down' is about to happen. Before that point, decisions have to be made on whether:
- All work continues up to the go/no point
- Some work like the Artist's continues
- Just the Leadership continues
- Or whether everyone is returned to their homeroom.

Sources of Drama:

- Getting people back after PMs have returned them to their professional communities is difficult. Functional Managers typically do not have overhead job numbers waiting and need their staff to be engaged in productive work. Both lines of the conversation below are not atypical for a PM to have within days or hours of each other.
    o "We are shutting down, take them back!"
    o "We just got approved, I need them back now!"

Best Practices:

- Now is the time to leverage your discussions with the Latte Benefactor.
    o If the Project is unlikely to reach the Benefactors' cost and schedule goals without great difficulties, there is less pressure to keep work going, particularly if you are close to having exhausted authorized funds. Seek guidance from the Latte Benefactor, as to whether you should prepare for a permanent shutdown.
    o If the Project is likely to reach the Benefactors' cost and schedule goals without great difficulties, seek guidance on whether unused funding should be employed to keep the Team together, progress design and engineering work, or some subset of it. If available funding is insufficient to maintain progress, seek guidance as to whether some type of 'bridge' funding can be assumed to avoid loss of momentum.

OBTW:

Don't assume 'bridge funding is a go' without clear signals from the Latte Benefactor on the specific amount and purpose.

3.3 – NEGOTIATIONS – REMEMBER, YOU ARE HANDCUFFED TO SOMEONE

Background:

Projecting the costs associated with the next round of effort will require the PM to negotiate services with all the functional areas.

Sources of Drama:

- When a PM is relatively new with no or few projects under their belt, it is difficult for them to have an opinion on how much something should cost or time that it should take. In this situation they may just default to:
    - o   The first pricing is always too high.
    - o   Or, just accepting the first number on good faith alone.

Best Practices:

- Whether you are a Newbie or deeply experienced PM:
    - o   Look at the historic costs for the last six jobs each functional area did. They may be similar or all very different. You goal is to see if there is a pattern in the cost (e.g., a consistent percentage against hard cost).
    - o   Then, look at the Projects most similar to yours, even if it extends deeper into the past, and see if there is a pattern. By doing all the above, you may find a pattern, but at a minimum you will have a hi/lo range for the functional area costs.

OBTW:

As a PM, your obligation is to also spot shortfalls in the functional areas' estimates. If your analysis, experience, or gut tells you they are short – have a reality check discussion with them. They may not have thought the job through, missed something, or are overly optimistic. If you let those circumstances go forward, all you have done is handcuff yourself to someone who is going to jump over a cliff of cost and schedule woes.

3.4 – CONSENSUS: TO SIGN OR NOT TO SIGN? THAT IS THE QUESTION

Background:

Some sort of formal or informal signal of consensus has to be established by the Team to confirm, "We are there."

Signing a cover sheet approving a list of the key documents produced in this phase is one way to do it.

Sources of Drama:

- Resistance is borne at the first mention of signing, and if not addressed, it can become a troublesome source of tension between the PM and the Team.
  - o The Artist fears that any signature would lock the design prematurely,
  - o Operations fears that the available high-level documents do not state their detailed requirements adequately,
  - o May feel or say,
    - "This is the first Project I have had to sign anything like this."
    - "Why are you the only PM doing this?"
    - "Can't we just say we are good to go?"
    - "You are going to hold this against me."
    - "I have never done a sign-off before."

Best Practices:

- The purpose of the sign-off should be stated in the fewest words possible, and be unique to each phase. For this phase it could easily be:
  - o Signature represents consensus that the accompanying documents are a snapshot suitable for summarizing and presenting the Project's findings on gross scope, function, cost, and technical viability to the Benefactors.

- This topic is not something to introduce to the Team at the last minute. The PM should introduce it early on in one on one sessions with the Artist, Operators, Estimator, and any other signatory party.

- The PM should be the first to sign, and if the Artist wants to be the last – that's okay.

- If there are exceptions that cannot be bridged by the Benefactor meeting, but they do not justify delaying the meeting, record and attach them to the signature page.

- Allow several days for people to visit the documents and sign them. If problems arise that prevent someone from signing you will have given yourself some time to resolve whatever is preventing them from doing so.

- Include the signature document and any exceptions with the materials submitted to the Benefactors.

OBTW:

Unless the company has institutionalized signing this approach is optional, and not a hill anyone should die on. It was my personal preference, as I have found it flushed-out issues that would otherwise show up as latent problems.

One of the most common problems with this approach, sometimes arising from the Operator side, was not including detailed information in the current phase. An example of this was design criteria on the number of shelves in a custodial closet. As the PM I thanked the source for the info, informed them that this information was not actionable for the current phase, but we would attach it to the sign-off docs as something that would be addressed downstream. With this, the Operator agreed there was no reason not to sign-off based on the information not being incorporated into the current drawings.

I also found that once the Team collectively steps across the first signature milestone, it is much easier to conduct this process at the end of the phases that follow, particularly if you never pull someone's signature out and hold it against them downstream.

In addition to the problems forced into the open, I found it shored up people's expectation that they had to make a commitment at the end of each phase, until fabrication and construction documents were complete.

3.5 - QUALITY CONTROL: PROOF READERS

Background:

No matter how good an engineer is, no bridge in the United States is engineered by solely one individual.

Sources of Drama:

- Missed opportunities to <u>stress test</u> the Big Idea technically, financially, or commercially arise from, "I don't need, have the money, or time for someone to check my work."

Best Practices:

- Like a writer, Artists, Designers, Engineers, and even Project Managers need 'proof readers' for their work – a trusted individual with a keen eye and honest perspective from outside the Team's ranks. This fresh set of eyes could bring something forward that the Artist or Designer has been looking at for months, but not seeing. Or, they may poke at a sacred cow or two that others were afraid to touch. Just having a viewpoint does not make these proof readers right, but their input can help balance the Team's sometimes blind bias in favor of the Project.
    - o   Mentors within your community make great 'proof readers.'

- For some Meyers Briggs personalities, the proof-reading process takes place casually as work moves along. These individuals like to expose their work to others and get energy from it, "Look what I did, Mom." For other personality types, the preference is to sequester themselves with no one looking over their shoulder. They lose energy by eyes peering into their progress. In either case, both types need to find a constructive way for the right set of eyes to confidentially preview the design, strategy, calculations, and other conclusions before the milestone version is unveiled to Benefactors.

OBTW:

You need others from outside the Team to try and <u>de-stabilize</u> your work to ensure it can pass muster before the Benefactors attempt to do so.

3.6 - QUALITY CONTROL: READ WHAT YOU PUT IN FRONT OF OTHERS

Background:

The PM will approach the final Benefactor presentation with a checklist of required documents.

Sources of Drama:
- Technical and credibility problems arise, when the Benefactors actually read and find problems with documents the PM failed to read prior to the presentation.
  - Checklists can provide PMs with a false sense of security that everything needed is present and right.
  - Relying on 'proof readers' is not enough because they don't know everything the PM knows.

Best Practices:

- There is no alternative to the PM reviewing everything being put in front of the Benefactors.

OBTW:

Another Frank (Stanek) moment involved a major scope summary that we were about to publish to our partner company. The associated binder held more than three hundred pages of detail that had taken several months to assemble. Frank had received the final draft, and I had innocently assumed that he would not have time to dive into the detail, and I had also assumed that my 'gross' review was an adequate last line of defense. I was wrong, and so was my presumption that the document was perfect.

Frank called me into his conference room where he had the document on the table. He said, "We have a few things we need to tighten up, before we send this," and then went on to quickly flag numerous pages, where he had bent the corners.

Frank's personal perusal of detail and quiet signal that he was looking at the work being produced, ensured that a much better job would be done by me, before future documents were put in front of him.

3.7 – EQUILIBRIUM – DON'T GET USED TO IT

Background:

Except for re-baselining moments that may have occurred earlier in this phase, most Projects will have been out of equilibrium the entire time. That is, instead of an equilateral triangle where scope, schedule, and budget are seemingly in calm balance, the Team has been wrestling with a scalene or isosceles triangle at best (e.g., too much scope, not enough money or time).

Sources of Drama:

- Even if a Team achieves balance between scope, schedule, and budget for the final Benefactor presentation, every leg of that equilateral triangle is like a spring in compression waiting for release.

- The natural state of things is to be out of balance, just as the Project was days before the final Benefactor presentation, and as it will return to within days after it (assuming it gets green lighted).

Best Practices:

- The PM is the Benefactor 'go to belly button' for determining whether the Big Idea's technical risk, and business proposition (i.e., scope, time, money) are compatible with each other. This responsibility entails delivering one of the following end states with the last two representing potential dream killers:
  o Achieve equilibrium by capturing the Artist's compelling vision within target budget and schedule, and with manageable technical risk.
  o Achieve equilibrium by capturing the Artist's compelling vision only through heroic assumptions on cost, schedule, and/or technical risk.
  o Not achieving equilibrium without options that significantly dilute the Artist's compelling vision in order to bring scope in line with tolerable cost, schedule, and risk targets.

- Presentation of the findings above always include:
  o The Team's recommended next steps and any related critical paths that require immediate action
  o Risk mitigation steps that need to be taken
  o Description of the next evolution of the Big Idea in artistic and technical form
  o And the 'ask' for next phase's schedule and funding.

OBTW:

If your pitch was successful you passed 'Go' and collected $200. You will now take another trip around the board with a new phase that also culminates in a Benefactor presentation, as the wet clay of the Big Idea continues its path to the kiln.

3.8 – CONCLUSION: "IS THAT REALLY YOU?"

Background:

The last item to share are two personal woulda, coulda, shoulda moments.

The first was the death of a fellow Imagineer. We bumped heads on occasion, but I had a lot of respect for his work and went to his funeral. While there, I learned from the eulogy that he and I were born in the same year, just a few days apart, and less than fifty miles separated his Midwest hometown from mine. I can guarantee that common history would have made me look and work with him differently.

The second involved a fellow retired Imagineer I crossed paths with at a lumber yard. We too had bumped heads in the past, but all that pressure was gone and we had a fantastic conversation.

In both cases above, I could not remember whether it was me, the other person, or both of us who had taken the stupid pills relative to grating on each other earlier in our careers. The trouble is, these late 'Kum ba yah' moments didn't do anything to help the Projects we had worked on together.

Sources of Drama:

- Lazy pills sometimes make it too easy to put one's thumb on the side of the scale that discounts the other person's value.

Best Practices:

- Be impatient! Don't wait for a funeral or post career lumber yard meeting to solve what may be bitter today.

- Bring forward the reality that time heals bruised feelings, and there is no reason not to restart a relationship. Restart it in the present, and behave in a way that your interaction with someone during the Project will be the same, as when you cross paths outside the fabric of a Project or your Company.

OBTW:

When all else fails, remember - Project Management is a fun job, but somebody has to do it!

AFTERWORD

Like a design, this book was iterated several times. The first words written were not the last words you read. Along these lines, it also had many draft titles including:
- WHAT THEY DIDN'T TEACH YOU IN SCHOOL
- LEADERSHIP IN THEME PARK DEVELOPMENT
- IT'S A FUN JOB, BUT SOMEBODY HAS TO DO IT
- THE CARE AND FEEDING OF THE DESIGN PROFESSIONAL
- THE ART OF THE POSSIBLE
- (ALMOST) EVERYBODY IS A PROJECT MANAGER
- HEALTHY DESIGN ITERATION
- TAKING THE DRAMA OUT OF THEMATIC DESIGN
- DRAMA VS. WISDOM IN THEMATIC DESIGN
- IS IT ART, OR IS IT A PROJECT?

Each candidate title was a puzzle piece for the body of content. Ultimately, they all merged, and fell easily under a Project Management umbrella fixed on the development of a Theme Park in its early life. However, the concepts shared could easily expand into resorts, exhibits, Expos, and the other branches of thematic design.

For you, this book started with your seeking it out. And it ends with you too, as it is your choice, as to which pieces of wisdom you draw upon. It is also your choice to discount what has been said here by dividing by three or embrace the knowledge and multiply its usefulness by ten. In either case, the following yardsticks can be used to measure your success in helping your Team achieve Great Team status:
- The Big Idea got even more compelling
- The Team was not afraid of iteration
- Those at the intersection of the Project and professional communities knew that they were also a project manager (small p, small m)
- The Big Idea met or surpassed all technical, operational, and commercial thresholds
- And the Team aggressively resisted conflict with each other.

I wish you the best of luck in your leadership endeavors, as you transition art into a project.

ABOUT THE AUTHOR

Val Usle is a former Walt Disney Imagineer with over four decades of service to the Company. During that time, he touched most of Imagineering's domestic and international projects (e.g., EPCOT, Tokyo Disneyland, Disneyland Paris, Indiana Jones, Toontown, Tokyo DisneySea, and Star Wars: Galaxy's Edge) in leadership roles as a Project Manager, Design Manager, Project Architect, Sustainable Design Executive, and Functional Manager (he led the Architecture, Show Set, Interiors, and Specifications Directorate).

Val Usle is an architect, and lives in a home he designed and built in Sierra Madre, California. He is also in the California State Guard, and serves as the S5 Planning Officer for a Special Operations Detachment. Additionally, he is a certified trainer of other architects and engineers in building damage assessment and was deployed to Hurricane Katrina and the Sonoma Fires.

After retiring from Imagineering, Val started Kimble Creek Consulting, LLC which focuses on coaching and helping owners mobilize their themed entertainment projects. He can be reached at valusle.kimblecreek@gmail.com.

THEME PARK PROJECT MANAGEMENT is Val's first work of non-fiction. His first book, PRAIRIE FIRE, was published in 1999. It is a novel of contemporary politics set in the American Midwest.

Made in United States
Orlando, FL
18 May 2025

61381649R00096